RAINY DAY PLAY!

Nancy Fusco Castaldo

Illustrations by Loretta Braren

WILLIAMSON PUBLISHING • CHARLOTTE, VERMONT 05445

Library of Congress
Cataloging-in-Publication Data

Fusco Castaldo, Nancy. 1962-
    Rainy day play!: explore, create, discover, pretend /
Nancy Fusco Castaldo.
    p. cm. — (A little hands book : 5)
    Includes index.
    ISBN 1-885593-00-7 (alk.paper)
    1. Creative activities and seat work. 2. Amusements.
I.Title.   II. Series: Williamson little hands book: 5.
  GV1203.F85 1996
    790.1'922—dc20   95-50477
                                              CIP

Cover and interior design: Trezzo-Braren Studio
Illustrations: Loretta Braren
Printing: Capital City Press

Williamson Publishing Co.
Box 185
Charlotte, Vermont 05445
(800) 234-8791

Books by Nancy Fusco Castaldo
Sunny Days & Starry Nights
A Little Hands Nature Book

CONTENTS

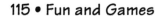

For my family

Acknowledgments

A special thanks to my parents for their constant love and support.

And again, to Susan and Jack Williamson for their continued faith and encouragement.

BRIGHT THOUGHTS ABOUT RAINY DAYS

A Note to Grown-Ups

Rainy days present challenges to adults with children in their care, whether parent, grandparent, caregiver, or teacher. But, it can be a positive challenge, as rainy days create wonderful opportunities for precious, shared time.

We all have days when we have to pop a video in the VCR. But, when time is available and the videos have gotten old, consider reading a book or making up stories together, instead. If you were thinking of setting out coloring books and crayons, turn to some of the art activities in the Index (pages 141–142) that are almost as easy and mess free. And don't overlook the fact that what is tedious to you may be fascinating and valuable to preschoolers. Give them a chance to dust, stack some books, or put away the groceries. They'll love doing it and will be very proud, knowing that you gave them such a big responsibility.

The experiences suggested within may take as little or as much time as you would like. They are meant to provide a stepping stone to further ideas and fun that you will discover together. Each activity is multi-faceted, giving preschoolers experience with such things as numbers, letters, imagination, and directions. At this age, the process of creative thinking is as valuable as the outcome. Everyone comes out a winner!

Who knows? Maybe rainy days will become favorite days just because they force us to slow down a bit, so we can share time and space, and giggles and learning with little ones.

COZY CORNER PLAY

When the rain is falling all around and your house is dry and safe, that is the time to nestle down and play and play and play!

IF I WERE

If you could be anything, what would you be? A giant-sized animal? Something that flies like an airplane? A truck driver? A tiny ant? Here's a chance to imagine being anything you like.

HERE'S WHAT YOU NEED

Open space

At least one other person

HERE'S WHAT YOU DO

1 Think of something or someone you would like to be — like an animal or a tree, or a mail delivery person or ballet dancer.

2 Now, without speaking, act out something that person or thing would do. For instance, "If I were a bird, I would fly through the sky." Let everyone guess what or who you are.

3 Take turns acting out and guessing.

CHIRP · CHIRP

LET IT POUR!

● How does it feel to be someone or something else? Can you imagine a whole day as that person or thing? Try being it for five minutes.

● Play Nursery Rhyme Charades. Take turns acting out your favorite nursery rhymes or storybook characters.

● Imagine that you are an animal outside in the rain. Do you like the rain or do you want to find protection?

COZY CORNER

Cinderella's cozy corner was near her fireplace. There she could imagine being in faraway places, read her favorite stories, or just curl up and listen to the raindrops falling on the roof. Cozy corners sure are special places!

THREE LITTLE PIGGIES

HERE'S WHAT YOU DO

1 Find a cozy place in your house — in a corner, under a table, or wherever. Place your blanket on the floor and pile on some pillows and maybe a stuffed animal or small toy car, too.

2 Sit in your cozy spot; listen to the rain. Is the raining coming down very **fast** and **hard**? Is it raining **gently**, with a comforting tap, tap, tap?

3 Enjoy your cozy corner. Color, play a game, hum softly to yourself, or have a nice warm cup of cocoa.

LET IT POUR!

● Listen to Jane Yolen's *Weather Report* for some great poems about weather.

● Talk about what makes you feel safe and cozy. When don't you feel safe and cozy?

● Try singing "Rain, Rain, Go Away" or "It's Raining, It's Pouring" as a round, while you listen to the rain fall outside.

MARATHON BOOK FESTIVAL

Celebrate books with your own marathon book festival! Invite a friend to join in the fun.

HERE'S WHAT YOU DO

1 Pick a subject to be the focus of your book festival. This is called the **theme**. You might pick trucks, dinosaurs, rabbits, or the seashore.

2 Search your shelves and books for stories and poems about your theme. Read them together with a grown-up.

3 Talk about the stories you read together and why you like some stories and maybe don't like other stories.

MAKE A BOOKMARK

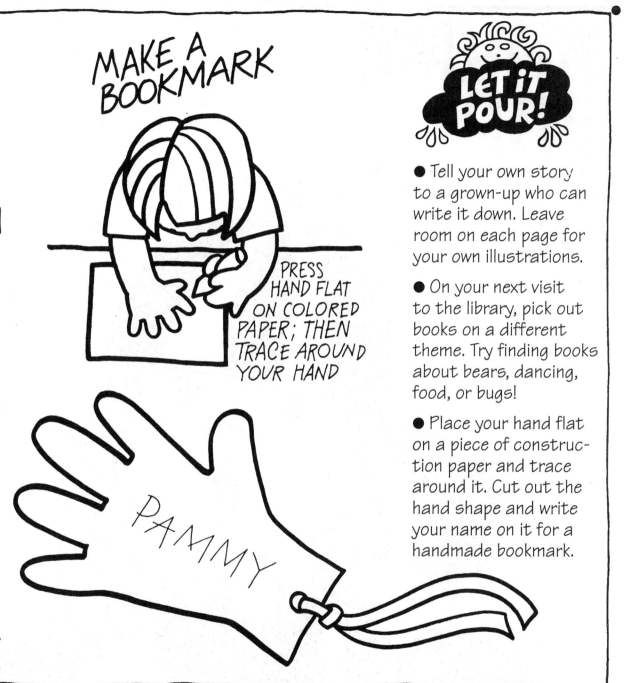

PRESS HAND FLAT ON COLORED PAPER; THEN TRACE AROUND YOUR HAND

PAMMY

LET iT POUR!

● Tell your own story to a grown-up who can write it down. Leave room on each page for your own illustrations.

● On your next visit to the library, pick out books on a different theme. Try finding books about bears, dancing, food, or bugs!

● Place your hand flat on a piece of construction paper and trace around it. Cut out the hand shape and write your name on it for a handmade bookmark.

RHYME RAP

Rhyming words, such as cat and hat or three and me, sound alike. It's fun to rhyme — if you've got the time!

THE CAT IN THE HAT SAT ON THE MAT

SNAP

SNAP · SNAP

HERE'S WHAT YOU DO

1 Read different kinds of poetry with a grown-up. Some poems rhyme and some poems don't. It is fun to listen for the rhyming words.

2 Say a word, any word (cat is a good one to start with). How many words can you think of that rhyme with your word?

LET IT POUR!

● Listen to some of these great poetry books: *Sing A Song of Popcorn* selected by Beatrice De Regniers, *Chicka Chicka Boom Boom* by Bill Martin, Jr., and *A Child's Garden of Verse* by Robert Louis Stevenson. Pick out your favorite poem.

● Start a rhyme journal. Cut out or draw pictures of rhyming words like a mouse and a house.

● Rhymes can lead to some very silly sayings. Make up a silly saying with rhyming words.

● Play a rhyming game. One person says a word like "red" and the other says a rhyme like "I sat on my bed." Listen to *What Rhymes with Eel?* by Harriet Ziefert.

LIGHTNING BOLT!

When we use a word to imitate a sound like buzz, hiss, or vroom! vroom!, we are using words to bring a sound to life. In poetry this is called **onomatopoeia**. What other words copy the sound something makes?

MOO, BAA, LA LA LA

Children in England play a game very similar to this. Do you think a cow says moo in far-off countries like England?

KIKIRIKI

MOO · MOO
MO · MO
BAAAH · BAAAH

OINK · OINK
BU · BU

HERE'S WHAT YOU NEED

Good, strong voices!
(the more the merrier)

HERE'S WHAT YOU DO

1 Everybody picks an animal with a special animal noise like moo or neigh.

2 A grown-up makes up a story including all of the animals. When you hear the name of your animal, make that animal's sound.

3 If the storyteller says "zoo," then all the animals make their noises together.

LET IT POUR!

● Talk about animal sounds in other countries. If you know someone who speaks another language, ask how to describe the sound a cow or a dog makes. Is it moo or bow wow?

● Look in a book or in old *National Geographic* magazines for pictures of animals in other parts of the world. Do they look the **same** or **different** from the animals you see outdoors?

● In North America, many people have dogs, cats, birds, or fish for pets. Ask someone who has lived or traveled in another part of the world what kinds of pets children have there?

LIGHTNING BOLT!

In the United States, cows seem to say moo moo, ducks say quack quack, and pigs say oink oink.

Children in Japan describe animal sounds differently. There, ducks say ga ga, cows say mo mo, chickens say piyo piyo, and pigs say bu bu.

In Rwanda, dogs say wu, wu, wu and roosters say guglug, guglug, guglug. African cats say miyau, miyau and cows say baaah, baaah, baaah.

In Italy, ducks say qua, qua. German roosters don't say cocka-doodle-doo; they say kikiriki.

Now here is a very tricky question: Do you think the animals make different sounds or do people just describe them differently depending on where they grow up?

GOING BATTY!

If you go outdoors on a summer's night, you'll probably see some bats overhead, as they hunt for mosquitoes. Don't be afraid; bats rarely go near people. They're too busy finding their dinner!

CUT OUT TWO BLACK CIRCLES

ZIGZAG CUT ONE CIRCLE IN HALF

GLUE HALF CIRCLE WINGS ON EACH SIDE OF BAT BODY

PUNCH HOLE IN TOP AND ATTACH YARN TO HANG

HERE'S WHAT YOU NEED

Black construction paper

Safety scissors

White craft glue

Yarn

HERE'S WHAT YOU DO

1 Ask a grown-up to help you cut two circles of the same size out of the construction paper.

2 Cut one circle in half, using a zigzag cut.

3 To create bat wings, glue a half circle to each side of the whole circle. Attach a piece of yarn to hang your bat.

● Some people think that bats are a kind of bird, but they are not. What is the **same** about a bird and a bat, and what is **different**? Listen to *Stellaluna* by Janell Cannon to hear about a fruit bat that lived with a bird family.

● Learn all about bats in *The Kids' Wildlife Book* by Warner Shedd. You can even learn a bat radar game and how to make a roosting bat.

SOUND WAVE SIGNALS

ECHOES BOUNCE BACK

LIGHTNING BOLT!

Bats hunt for their food using a system almost like radar. They send out sound wave signals and then, depending on how the sound waves bounce back, they can tell how near something is. This system is so finely tuned that bats can find flying mosquitoes. In fact, each bat eats about 600 mosquitoes in about an hour! Now, that's a bat with a big appetite.

MY SPECIAL LETTERS

Words come alive, just wait and see.
There's so much more than A, B, C.

Extra snapshot

Old magazines

Construction paper

Safety scissors

Glue stick

Marker

Clear contact paper

HERE'S WHAT YOU DO

1 Your initials are the first letter of your first, last, and middle names. If your name is **John Stanley Greene**, your initials are **JSG**.

2 Ask a grown-up to help you write down and sound out your initials.

3 Starting with the letter of your first name, cut out pictures that begin with that letter's sound. Draw the letter nice and big on a piece of construction paper and then glue all the pictures around the letter.

PAGES

GLUE ON ONE INITIAL THEN PICTURES THAT HAVE INITIAL'S SOUND

4 Do the same thing for each of your initials. Now you have a book of your initial sounds.

5 To make a cover, trace your initials on a piece of paper and glue your photograph on it.

6 Punch holes in your pages and tie them together with a piece of yarn.

PUNCH HOLES IN COVER AND PAGES THEN TIE WITH YARN

COVER

GLUE ON INITIALS AND PICTURE OF YOURSELF

LET iT POUR!

- If you can spell your first name, make a book with each letter's alphabet sounds.

- Ask a friend or two to help you make an alphabet book. Each of you take certain letters of the alphabet and cut out pictures with that letter's sounds.

- Look at other alphabet picture books. *Pigs From A to Z* by Arthur Geisert and *Amazon Alphabet* by Tanis Jordan are just two that are wonderful to read together.

OUTDOOR RAINY DAY FUN!

All rainy days don't have to be inside days. On days that are warm with a light rain falling, you might be able to venture outdoors for awhile. Oh, what fun it will be!

PUDDLE WALK

• •

A gentle rain is falling and you are dressed in your boots and your slicker. (Or maybe it is very warm and you can go outside in your bathing suit!) Here's some fun for days that are wet and drippy.

HERE'S WHAT YOU DO

1 Dress according to the out-door temperature and then take a rainy day walk around your yard or down the street with a grown-up.

2 There may not be many people outdoors, but there is certain to be a lot of critters out and about. Look for **worms** that come out of the ground during the rain and end up on walkways. Look for **spider webs** covered with raindrops. Are you surprised that the rain hasn't washed away the webs?

3 Examine raindrops that sit like tiny bubbles on leaves or railings with your hand lens.

4 How does the rain feel? Stick out your tongue and catch a raindrop. Touch leaves, soil, and rocks. Feel the squishy ground beneath your feet.

LET IT POUR!

● Talk about the difference between summer rainy days and fall rainy days.

● Play I Spy in the rain. Each player picks something for the other player to find. For example, "I spy a leaping frog" or "I spy a slippery leaf."

● Look for rainy day critters like snails, frogs, toads, and salamanders. Then, go indoors, dry off, and listen to *The Salamander Room* by Anne Mazer.

● Look for rainbows just as the sun begins to burst forth.

DRIP DROP

Drip drop, pitter patter, ping pong! The sounds of raindrops have many voices. Let's listen together.

PING

PONG

PANG

HERE'S WHAT YOU DO

1 Dress according to the weather. Place the containers upside down, one at a time in the rain. What sound does the rain make as it falls on each container?

2 Add groups of containers to create your own rainy day chorus. Which containers make the loudest sound?

3 Turn some containers right side up. Does the sound change as the containers begin to fill up with water?

4 Place some of the containers under a heavier drip, like rain dripping off the edge of the roof. Is the sound different?

LET IT POUR!

● Use the containers to measure the rainfall. Which containers fill up more quickly? Use a ruler to measure how much rain has fallen into each container. Why do the amounts differ?

● Listen to the weather report to find out how much rain actually fell for that day. Which container measured the closest amount?

● Listen to *Cloudy with a Chance of Meatballs* and *Return to Chewandswallow* by Judi Barrett. Then, pretend you are collecting food instead of raindrops in your containers.

PLAY LEAP FROG

Bend those legs and jump like a frog! How high can you jump? Leap frog is so much fun.

HERE'S WHAT YOU DO

1 Find an open area on the grass. Have one player squat down.

2 With your hands on the player's back, leap over him or her.

3 Set up a long line of jumpers. The person on the end jumps over everyone else and finishes in a squatting position in the front.

4 Make frog noises as you play. Ribbit! Ribbit!

LET IT POUR!

● With a grown-up, take a walk around a pond to watch some real frogs leaping.

● To meet some wonderful frogs and toads, listen to Arnold Lobel's frog and toad stories.

● Can't go outdoors today? Play leap frog inside and leap from room to room.

RIBBIT · RIBBIT

LIGHTNING BOLT!

Did you know that frogs and toads are not the same? Almost all toads have bumpy, warty, earth-colored skin; frogs are known to have smooth, green skin. You will see more frogs near the water. Toads spend most of their time on land (you might even find one living in a flowerpot).

Toads generally do more hopping and are sometimes called hoptoads. Frogs are mostly leapers. Try hopping like a toad and leaping like a frog!

SPLISH! SPLASH! GIVE A PLANT A BATH!

A gentle rainfall is the perfect time to give your indoor houseplants a much-needed shower. They'll thank you for it by growing healthier.

HERE'S WHAT YOU NEED

Indoor plants

Cotton swabs

A gentle rain

HERE'S WHAT YOU DO

1 Place your plants outside.

2 Let your plants enjoy the light rain shower. Use cotton swabs to clean leaves and any mites (they look like specks of cotton).

3 After about a half hour, shake your plants slightly to remove extra water before taking them back inside.

4 Place your plants in a bathtub, sink, or on a counter to let them dry before setting them back in their original places in the house.

5 Don't your plants look refreshed?

LET iT POUR!

- Watch the water fall on the leaves. Does the water sit on the leaf or roll right off?

- Clean off any dead leaves from your plant.

- Help a grown-up repot a plant that has grown too big for its pot.

- Many leaves are **dark green**, but some are **bright green, red, purple,** and even **striped** in two colors. What colors are your plants' leaves?

LIGHTNING BOLT!

Do you know why it is so important to give your plants a shower? Plants actually breathe through their leaves — not by taking deep breaths like you and me, but by absorbing fresh air through their leaves. So, if the leaves are dusty, it is harder for them to breathe.

PUDDLE POWER

Jump in a puddle and splash about. Where will it go? Let's find out.

HERE'S WHAT YOU NEED

Chalk

Puddles

HERE'S WHAT YOU DO

1 After a rainfall, take a walk outside to find puddles. Draw a chalk outline around each puddle (or outline it with a mark drawn with a stick in the soil).

2 What sounds do you hear after the rain stops? Do you hear water dripping? Birds singing? It is a wonderful time to be outdoors.

3 Now, go back to your puddle and watch what happens to it as the ground begins to dry. How did your puddle change?

LET IT POUR!

● Watch birds enjoy the puddles after a rainfall. What are they doing?

● Try skipping stones on a big puddle.

● Make a paper toy boat and float it on a puddle after the rain stops. Or, float a leaf on the puddle.

LIGHTNING BOLT!

Where do you think the water in the puddle went? If you guessed that it dried up, you are partially correct. The water did dry up, but it didn't disappear. It actually was heated up by the sun and, in drops even smaller than raindrops, it floated back up toward the sky again. This is called **evaporation**. Now, do you want to know something really curious? When it rains somewhere else, some of those same drops of water that evaporated will fall back to earth again, perhaps into a new puddle.

MUDPIES, WEEDS, and SEEDS

Some people say you shouldn't garden in the rain, but for little hands there is no better time because the earth is warm and moist.

Gloves

Old clothes

1 Wear appropriate clothing for a muddy day. The ground is nice and soft when it rains, making it a great time to help a grown-up pull up the weeds. Gently pull from just above the ground so the roots come out, too.

2 Take a close look at the roots, stem, and, if there is one, weed flower. Notice if the root is long and thick, or if there are a lot of tiny roots.

3 Here's a curious question: Is there a difference between a weed and a flower that is left to grow in the garden?

4 When a soft rain is falling, it's also a great time for planting. The ground is soft and can easily be dug to make room for seeds or new plants. And remember, you won't have to water!

● Besides weeds, there are other pests that people try to keep out of gardens. Listen to *The Tale of Peter Rabbit* to learn about one such critter who couldn't stay out of a vegetable garden.

● What's a summer rain without mudpies? Make mudpies with the wet soil. Decorate them with leaves, sticks, pebbles, and flowers. Set them out to bake when the sun comes out.

ART SMART!

Some people think of rainy days as dull, gray days. It doesn't have to be that way, of course. You can fill your rainy days with lots of bright colors and fun things to do!

WHO NEEDS A BRUSH?

You don't need a paintbrush to paint a great picture. In fact, sometimes it's even more fun without one!

HERE'S WHAT YOU NEED

Newspaper

Container of water

Egg carton

Finger-paint paper

Washable tempera paint

All sorts of possible painting tools

HERE'S WHAT YOU DO

1 Collect old toothbrushes, toothpicks, feathers, straws and other things that might make unusual painting tools. Cover the table with newspaper.

2 Pour the paint into the egg carton sections.

3 Experiment with your tools and your paint. Do you get lots of thin lines with a toothbrush and a big fat line with a cotton swab? What tool can you use to paint animal fur?

4 Paint your own masterpiece!

● Talk about the appearance of different **textures** you created with your painting tools. Which ones look **smooth**? **Rough**?

● Make mystery rubbings of objects around your house or classroom with crayons. What surface works best for your rubbings — rough or smooth? Ask someone to guess where the rubbing came from.

LIGHTNING BOLT!

Artists apply their paints using many different tools, just as you did. They also create different effects by using various kinds of paint like water-colors or oils and by using different kinds of paper like rice paper or canvas. Do you have a favorite way to draw using crayons, markers, or paints?

STAINED-GLASS RAINDROPS

While you are watching the falling rain, you can make your own raindrops to hang on your windows.

HERE'S WHAT YOU DO

1 Ask a grown-up to cut the plastic sheet in half. Then, draw the shape of a raindrop on the plastic. Layer the two plastic halves and cut out two identical raindrops.

2 Lay one raindrop flat on a table. Take a pea-sized or smaller piece of the beeswax in your hand. Roll it around, warming it up in your hands, softening it.

3 Press the beeswax onto the plastic. Continue adding beeswax pieces until the entire raindrop is filled with multi-colored flat pieces of wax.

4 Place the other plastic raindrop on top of the wax. Press the sheet onto the wax, sticking the two sides together.

5 Ask a grown-up to punch a hole in the top of the raindrop so you can hang it from a window. Now even on the rainiest day you can still have some color shining in your window!

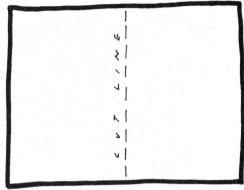

CUT PLASTIC SHEET IN HALF

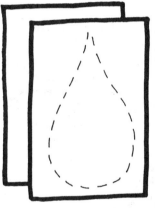

DRAW RAINDROP ON ONE HALF OF PLASTIC, STACK ON OTHER HALF AND CUT OUT

PRESS DOWN WARM PIECES OF BEESWAX ON ONE RAINDROP

PRESS OTHER RAINDROP SHAPE ON TOP OF WAX

LET iT POUR!

● Use the plastic sheets and beeswax to make a variety of stained-glass shapes. Try hearts and diamonds — even your initials!

● The next time you are in the grocery store look for honey still in a honeycomb. If you can buy it, take it home, look at how the bees made it, and then eat some honey.

ALMOST BATIK

Sometimes making art means using unusual methods. Here's something very unusual that turns out very nicely.

HERE'S WHAT YOU DO

1 Draw a picture with crayons on white paper.

2 Place your picture in water. After a few minutes, gently remove the paper and crumble it into a ball.

3 Then, open up the paper and place it flat on the newspaper. Paint all over the entire sheet with your watercolor paint. Dip the picture back into the water for a quick minute.

4 Remove the picture and place flat to dry on the newspaper.

LET IT POUR!

● What part of the directions for Almost Batik seemed unusual to you?

● Create an ocean picture by drawing fish and other marine critters with your crayons. Paint over the entire picture with watered-down blue watercolor paint. See how the waxy crayons keep the blue paint off.

LIGHTNING BOLT!

Batik is an art originally used by the people of Java to decorate cloth. The artist uses hot wax to make a design, like the crayon does in the activity. The cloth is then dyed. The dye clings to the unwaxed areas of the cloth, leaving the waxed areas white. Later, the wax is scraped or boiled off the fabric and the design appears.

DINNER IS SERVED!

Set yourself up for some fun — and get ready to set the dinner table, too! You can make some festive woven place mats for a dinnertime surprise!

HERE'S WHAT YOU NEED

Construction paper

Safety scissors

Stapler or glue

HERE'S WHAT YOU DO

1 Ask a grown-up to help you cut the construction paper lengthwise into strips for weaving.

2 Arrange four strips into a square border for your place mat. Ask a grown-up to help you staple or glue the corners forming a square.

3 Next, glue or staple strips across the square to create a base for your weaving.

4 Weave strips of construction paper over and under the base strips. Finish by gluing or stapling down the ends.

LET IT POUR!

● Set the table with your colorful place mats. Add forks to the left of the plate and spoons to the right.

● Make a centerpiece for the table. It could be a small teddy bear, some wildflowers, or an arrangement of fresh fruits and vegetables.

LIGHTNING BOLT!

People in other parts of the world have different dining traditions and eating utensils. Learn how people in other countries set their tables for dinner. Try eating with chopsticks as some Asian people do, or set dinner on a coffee table and sit on pillows in the style of Japanese dining.

WACKY HATS

It may not be the right hat for a walk in the rain, but this will surely turn heads when you wear it!

HERE'S WHAT YOU DO

1 Ask a grown-up to cut about 2"–3" (5 cm-7.5 cm) straight across the bottom of the plate. Next, cut out the center.

2 Try on the plate for size. It should fit like a headband.

3 Cut out shapes from construction paper and glue to the plate.

4 Decorate the hat with streamers, glitter, flowers — or whatever to make the wackiest hat ever.

GLUE DECORATIONS ON PLATE RING

LET IT POUR!

● Put your Wacky Hat on and listen to *Jennie's Hat* by Ezra Jack Keats, *Caps for Sale* by Esphyr Slobodkina, and Dr. Seuss's *The Cat in the Hat.*

● Take an old hat and dress it up with feathers, silk flowers, ribbons, and any other decorations.

● Make a "Just-For-You" gift hat with special decorations like golf tees for someone who golfs or Lego™ blocks and small toys for a friend.

● Cheer up someone at school or at home. Make a courtly crown out of construction paper, decorate it with glitter and sequins, and name that person king or queen for the day.

CEREAL MOSAIC

You don't need much to create this masterpiece — just look at your cereal bowl and let your imagination soar!

HERE'S WHAT YOU DO

1 Spread some craft glue on the back of the construction paper and glue it to the cardboard. Let dry.

2 Dip the toothpick into the glue. Using the toothpick like a pencil, draw a shape, design, or letter on the paper. Fill in the shape with glue, too, if you choose.

3 Place cereal pieces close together, wherever you have glue. Allow the mosaic to dry.

GLUE

LET IT POUR!

● While you are making your mosaic, name all the kinds of cereal you can think of. Then, name only the ones you like. How many do you like?

● What other breakfast foods can you name? Talk about why breakfast is important.

● Use dried beans, rice, and macaroni to make another mosaic picture.

CRAZY CRITTER

Have fun sculpting your own Crazy Critter!

HERE'S WHAT YOU NEED

Egg carton, yogurt cups

White craft glue

Pipe cleaners

Sequins, buttons, or beads

Safety scissors

HERE'S WHAT YOU DO

1 Spread your materials in front of you. Do you see the makings for a Crazy Critter?

2 Remember Crazy Critters come right from your imagination. Use sections of the egg carton to make a caterpillar-type body or a roly-poly body.

3 Attach pipe cleaners for arms, legs, antennae — or for crazy hair! Use the glue to assemble your sculpture.

CRAFT GLUE

 LET IT POUR!

● Read about imaginary creatures in Dr. Seuss's books. Pick a name for your critter and make up a story about it.

● Ask a grown-up to make a batch of salt dough or baking soda clay. Sculpt a wacky animal or pet.

● Visit a museum or look at books to search out sculpture. Look for Rodin's masterpieces and ballerina sculptures by Degas.

ARMADILLO

LIGHTNING BOLT!

There are some very unusual, real animals whose appearances might surprise you. Go to a zoo, if you can, or look in some animal books or *National Geographic* magazines at the library. Do you see anything unusual like an **armadillo** in its suit of armor or a **rhinoceros** wallowing in the mud? Even the graceful **giraffe** is quite a surprising creature!

SNIP ART

Here's some art fun in the Japanese style of paper folding and cutting.

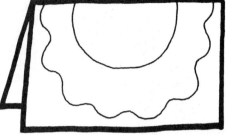

FOLD PAPER IN HALF, DRAW AND CUT OUT BRACELET—OPEN AND DECORATE

HERE'S WHAT YOU NEED

Origami paper or squares of wrapping paper

Safety scissors

Pencil

HERE'S WHAT YOU DO

1 Fold a paper square in half. Draw a half circle about 3 inches (7.5 cm) on the folded edge. Around the circle draw a scalloped border.

2 Cut out the outside scalloped edge and then the inside part of the half-circle, creating a fancy bracelet when opened.

MAKE A SNOWFLAKE

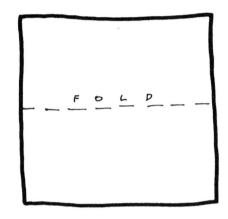

F O L D

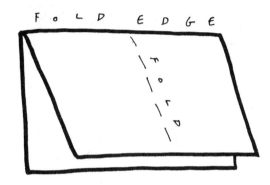

F O L D   E D G E

F O L D

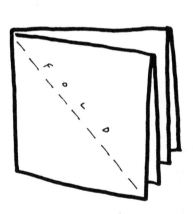

F O L D

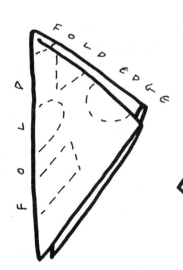

F O L D   E D G E

F O L D

LET iT POUR!

● Listen to *The Crane Wife* retold by Sumiko Yagawa and *Tree of Cranes* by Allan Say.

● Ask a grown-up to help you make a snowflake out of paper. Hang it from string in your window.

LIGHTNING BOLT!

Paper cutting is popular in many countries. *Kirigami* is the Japanese art of paper cutting (*kiri* means cutting and *gami* means paper in Japanese). In some European countries, very detailed designs of flowers, hearts, and birds are cut to decorate boxes and furniture. Some children in other countries are taught paper-cutting techniques in school.

GIGGLES ♥

and WIGGLES

Giggles seem to start with a grin and grow until laughter just comes spilling out. Here you'll find giggles, grins, silliness, and plenty of fun of every kind.

RAINY DAY BACKWARDS PARTY

We've all walked backwards, worn our baseball caps backwards, but have you ever done everything backwards? You're sure to have a giggling good time!

HERE'S WHAT YOU NEED

A few friends

Refreshments including sandwiches and dessert

Paper and crayons

Large mirror nearby

HERE'S WHAT YOU DO

1 Invite some friends over and ask them to wear their clothes backwards. Greet them at the door, saying "Good-bye."

2 Everyone print or trace their names on a piece of paper with crayons. Ask a grown-up to help. Then, hold the piece of paper in front of a mirror. What do you notice?

3 Next, serve a backwards meal — you guessed it, eating the dessert first! Eat with your opposite hand.

4 Tell riddles and knock, knock jokes — backwards! Give the answer first and ask your friends to make up the question or joke. When the party's over, say "Hello!"

• Make up a secret backwards language. Here's one way: Take a word like run. Add the sound "ay" to the end of every word. "Run to the store" becomes "Runay toay theay storeay." Now, you try it.

• Ask a grown-up to read you a favorite story beginning at the back of the book. Can you guess what is going to happen next?

Runay toay theay storeay. Okay Dokay!

LIGHTNING BOLT!

When you learn to read English, you will begin at the front of the book and read each line moving your eyes from left to right. In the Hebrew language, however, you would begin at the back of the book and read each line from right to left. So backwards in English is frontwards in Hebrew!

SILLY TONGUE TWISTERS

Does your tongue ever get twisted up so that funny words spill out of your mouth? Well, here are some tongue twisters that will give you the giggles!

HERE'S WHAT YOU NEED

Index cards

Markers

HERE'S WHAT YOU DO

1. Think of a silly tongue twister or make one up. Here are three to get you started:

   She sells sea shells at the seashore.
   Peter Piper picked a peck of pickled peppers.
   Rubber baby buggy bumpers.

2 Draw a picture that will remind you of it, like a picture of sea shells.

3 Ask a grown-up to write down the tongue twister on the back of the card.

4 Then, hold up a card. Can you remember the tongue twister from the picture? If not, a grown-up can read it. Everyone practice saying it together slowly.

5 After you have practiced a bit, go full speed ahead. How many times can you say your tongue twister without making an error? If you can say it more times than anyone else without making a mistake, you win that card. Then, go on to the next card.

The **ch**atty **ch**icken and the **ch**ummy **ch**imp rode on the **ch**oo **ch**oo.

● Make up your own tongue twisters. Think of words that start with the same letter. How fast can you say them?

● Make a tongue-twister collage. Cut out pictures of words that all begin with the same sound like **ch**icken, **ch**atty, **ch**imp, **ch**oo **ch**oo. Then make up a silly tongue twister using everything in your collage. "The chatty chicken and the chummy chimp rode on the choo choo."

BE A CLOWN

Here's your chance to really clown around!

HERE'S WHAT YOU NEED

Some oversized clothes
(ask a grown-up)

Paper plate

Markers

Yarn

1 Draw a clown face on the bottom of your paper plate with your markers. Ask a grown-up to poke a hole on each side of the plate for the yarn ties and eyeholes, too. Tie the yarn on.

2 Dress up in some big clothes. Tie your clown mask around your head.

3 Think about what a clown does to make people laugh. Try a dance or a song, do a somersault, plant a big kiss on someone's cheek, or just act goofy!

DRAW A CLOWN FACE
ON BOTTOM OF PAPER PLATE

POKE A HOLE ON EACH SIDE
OF PLATE AND ATTACH YARN

LET IT POUR!

● Look at the wonderful circus pictures in *Circus* by Peter Spier.

● Make your own paper plate tambourine. Jingle and jangle, stamp and shake, you'll be surprised at the music you make!

● Cut out huge clown feet from construction paper and ask a grown-up to help tie them to your feet.

KNOCK, KNOCK

Knock, knock. Whose there? Just me with a great knock, knock joke especially for you!

KNOCK · KNOCK ·

WHO'S THERE?

HERE'S WHAT YOU DO

1 Knock, knock jokes have a set pattern:

You: "Knock, knock."

They: "Who's there?"

You think of something funny to say like: "Banana."

They: "Banana, who?"

You finish your joke: "Banana split!"

2 Sit down with some friends and make up funny knock, knock jokes. Then draw a picture on the top of the page that reminds you of the joke. Ask a grown-up to write the joke on the bottom half of the page.

3 Punch holes in the side of the papers and tie with yarn for a great Knock, Knock Joke Book.

BANANA

JOKE BOOK

LET IT POUR!

● Instead of knock, knock jokes, collect riddles in a Riddle Book. Ask everyone at dinner to think of at least one funny riddle to add to your book.

● For a lot of giggles, read *Riddle-icious* by J. Patrick Lewis and *Why Did the Chicken Cross the Road And Other Riddles Old & New* by Joanna Cole.

SILLY STORY CIRCLE

Share a silly story with your friends and see who has the last word.

HERE'S WHAT YOU NEED

At least one other person

Your imagination

HERE'S WHAT YOU DO

1 Pick an animal or a person — like a bunny or a police officer — to be the main character in your story.

2 Because the story is going to be silly, quietly think of the silly things this character can do. Use your imagination.

3 One person begins the story by saying something about the character; then, the next person adds something to the story. Continue taking turns creating a story about the character. How silly can you make your story?

LET IT POUR!

● All the storytellers make up a title for the story and decide what would be on the cover of the storybook. Then, each of you draw your own storybook cover.

● No one to play Silly Story with? Start a silly story with a grown-up at home. See how long you can keep your story going. Continue adding a few sentences every day.

LIGHTNING BOLT!

Many books that you listen to contain stories that are **make-believe**. The story didn't really happen; it is **pretend**. Some books are about **true** things like a book about how a baby chick hatches. Sometimes it is hard to tell pretend stories and true stories apart. Ask a librarian to help you pick out one make-believe story and one true story.

SHAKE THE SILLIES OUT

Stomp like an elephant, sway like a tree, or just kick up your heels and dance to the beat!

HERE'S WHAT YOU NEED

A variety of music

Open space

HERE'S WHAT YOU DO

1 Listen to some music. Does the music make you think of something? How does it make you feel?

2 Move your body to the beat of the music. Does the music make you want to sway like an elephant's trunk, leap like a graceful deer, or fly like an airplane?

3 Go with the music, sway to the slow parts and gallop to the fast parts, changing as the music changes.

LET IT POUR!

● Pretend you are the wind. Move your body as if you are a warm summer breeze, then try to move like you are a howling wind storm. Try moving like other things: be water rushing down a stream, a gentle wave rolling on a sandy beach, or a light snowfall that turns into a blizzard!

● Watch the video *"Dance along with George Balanchine's The Nutcracker,"* (1993, Warner Home Video) and then — dance along!

PERFECTLY PREPOSTEROUS PARADE

Put on some marching music and strut your stuff!

HERE'S WHAT YOU DO

1 Put on some marching music and become the bandleader, the drummer, or the flag bearer in your own parade.

2 March from room to room. Stand tall and march to the beat.

HERE'S WHAT YOU NEED

Marching music

LET IT POUR!

● Make your own marching instruments. Try a pie tin drum, a rolled newspaper baton, or a bag-and-beans rhythm shaker to add to the music.

● Sing "The Ants Go Marching" as you parade through your house.

KITCHEN CONNECTION

The kitchen is a great place to explore, create, and have fun. Here are some good-time activities for you to enjoy and some yummy treats to eat, too.

SCRATCH and SNIFF PAINTING

Here's a way to make your painting look good — and smell good, too!

| Watercolor paints |
| Craft glue |
| Fruit-flavored gelatin |
| Paper |
| Paintbrush |

1 Place your paper on a sheet of newspaper. Use the watercolors to paint a fruity picture. Look at a bowl of apples and bananas to help you. Let your painting dry.

2 After your fruit picture is dry, spread the craft glue over each of your fruits. Sprinkle powdered, fruit-flavored gelatin over the wet craft glue.

3 Let your picture dry. The craft glue will dry clear and you will be left with a sweet-smelling picture!

LET IT POUR!

● How many different kinds of fruit can you name? Which ones are your favorites?

● Make a fruit salad with a grown-up. You can peel the bananas and wash the grapes, while someone else cuts the fruits. Toss and eat!

● Play a fruit guessing game. Someone names a fruit like strawberries, and everyone else names their favorite way to eat it like "on cereal" or "in ice cream" or "freshly picked from the fields."

LIGHTNING BOLT!

Depending on what part of North America you live in, you might have different fruit growing outside. Can you pick lemons from your trees? The answer is yes if you live in California. Is apple season a special time of year? It is if you live in Vermont, New York, or Washington. If you can pick a juicy orange right in your backyard, you may very well live in Florida.

BREAD PEOPLE

Here's a way to make your very own play people — out of bread! When they're finished they'll be great to play with, but too hard to eat.

HERE'S WHAT YOU NEED

1 cup (250 ml) water
1 cup (250 ml) salt
3 cups (750 ml) flour
Mixing bowl
Toothpicks
Garlic press

HERE'S WHAT YOU DO

1 Mix all the ingredients together in the mixing bowl.

2 Knead the dough until it's smooth. The dough should feel rubbery and smooth when it is ready to form into Bread People. Do you like the way it feels on your hands?

3 Make a ball from the dough for the body. Make a smaller ball for the head. Connect the two using a drop of water.

4 Roll the dough to make arms and legs. Press a small amount of dough through the garlic press to form hair. Attach the arms, legs, and hair to the body using a little water.

5 Add clothes using more dough and draw a face with a toothpick.

6 Ask a grown-up to bake your bread people in an oven for 2–3 hours at 275°F (140°C).

7 Let cool and paint with tempera paint, if you wish.

MIX WATER, SALT, FLOUR IN A BOWL

KNEAD THE DOUGH TILL SMOOTH

MAKE DOUGH BALLS FOR HEAD AND BODY

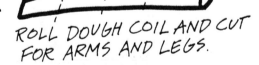

ROLL DOUGH COIL AND CUT FOR ARMS AND LEGS.

LET iT POUR!

● To make refrigerator magnets, cut out the dough with cookie cutters. (If the dough sticks to the cookie cutters, spray them with a no-stick cooking spray.) After they are baked, paint them, add glitter, and glue a magnet to the back.

● Make all kinds of Bread People and Bread Animals, wearing costumes and uniforms. How could you make the fur on a kitty?

● Listen to the story about the gingerbread boy and then make some gingerbread cookies for a yummy rainy day snack.

WINNIE-THE-POOH PICNIC

You don't need a sunny day for a picnic. Just spread a blanket inside and enjoy everything — except the ants!

HERE'S WHAT YOU NEED

Blanket

Peanut butter

Honey

Muffins

Winnie-the-Pooh books

HERE'S WHAT YOU DO

1 Spread your blanket on the floor. Ask a grown-up to help you spread the peanut butter and honey on your muffins. Bring along your favorite drinks.

2 Invite your stuffed animals to join your picnic. Read from your Winnie-the-Pooh books and watch the rain fall on the windowpanes. Pretend you are one of Pooh's friends on this rainy day. How would each one behave at the picnic?

LET IT POUR!

- Read the chapter of A.A. Milne's *Winnie-the-Pooh* titled "In Which Piglet Is Entirely Surrounded by Water."

- Make up your own melody and sing Pooh's song, "I'm Just a Little Black Rain Cloud."

- Christopher Robin used to watch the raindrops race down the window. Pick your own racing raindrops and watch to see which one wins the race to the windowsill.

LIGHTNING BOLT!

A.A. Milne wrote the Winnie-the-Pooh stories in 1926. Children of all ages have been listening to them ever since. Talk to some friends and talk to some older people, too, about their favorite adventures of Pooh and their favorite Pooh characters. Two wonderful collections of poems by A.A. Milne are *Now We Are Six* and *When We Were Very Young*. See if you can find them in the library.

BUTTER IN A JAR

You can make your very own butter — just as folks did long ago — and share it with your family for dinner or with classmates for a snack.

HERE'S WHAT YOU NEED

½ cup (125 ml) heavy cream
1 tablespoon (15 ml) sour cream
Lidded jar
Spoon
Saucer
Salt (optional)

HERE'S WHAT YOU DO

1 Pour the cream and sour cream into the jar.

2 Cover the jar tightly and shake it hard. Keep shaking or take turns shaking with a few people. Watch the liquids as you shake them up. After a long while, you will see a lump of soft butter at the bottom of the jar.

3 Pour off the leftover liquid and place the butter in a saucer. Press the butter firmly with the rounded back of a spoon, draining the water. (If you like salted butter, sprinkle some on the butter.) Guess what? You have made your own delicious butter!

POUR CREAM AND SPOON SOUR CREAM INTO JAR

SCREW ON LID AND SHAKE· SHAKE· SHAKE

WHEN LUMP FORMS POUR OUT LIQUID

PLACE BUTTER ON A SAUCER

PRESS WITH SPOON

LET IT POUR!

• Have a tea party serving tea, toast, your homemade butter, and jam!

• Listen to *Lucy's Christmas* and *Lucy's Summer* by Donald Hall to hear about other activities and games children played long ago.

STORYTIME CHEF

Ask a grown-up to help you plan a storybook meal and enjoy foods like green eggs and ham, along with angel food cake and chamomile tea.

HERE'S WHAT YOU NEED

Storybooks

A kitchen to work in

HERE'S WHAT YOU DO

1 Talk about some of your favorite books and stories. Pooh is always looking for honey, but what other foods do your storybook friends like to eat?

2 Did anyone mention Peter Rabbit's chamomile tea, Dr. Seuss's green eggs and ham, or the cakes Miss Spider serves at her tea party?

3 Plan a storybook menu with a main course, a drink, and some dessert. Have a pretend dinner with your friends acting out the characters in the stories. Who would you be at Miss Spider's tea party?

YUMMIE!

LET IT POUR!

• Would you like to eat green eggs and ham? Which storybook foods sound yummy and which ones sound yucky?

• What do you suppose Nancy Willard's book *High Rise Glorious Skittle Skat Roarious Sky Pie Angel Food Cake* is about? Listen to it to see if you are right. Now, make up your own funny food story with an equally funny title.

• Listen to *Possum Magic* by Mem Fox to discover foods like Pavlova, Vegemite, and Minties.

PERFECTLY EASY PRETZELS

Salty, doughy pretzels are a favorite treat for many people. Here's a pretzel with a little different twist!

HERE'S WHAT YOU NEED

Refrigerated biscuit dough

Cinnamon

Brown sugar

Cookie sheet

Rolling pin

HERE'S WHAT YOU DO

1 Using a rolling pin, roll out the refrigerated dough.

2 Ask a grown-up to cut the dough into long, fat strips.

3 Place two strips side by side and twist them together. Then, shape your pretzel into the traditional pretzel shape, your initials, or any other shape.

4 Sprinkle on the brown sugar and cinnamon, place on a cookie sheet, and bake following the package directions.

LET IT POUR!

● When you buy a bag of pretzels in the grocery store they are usually right next to the potato chips. What is the **same** about chips and pretzels and what is **different**?

● Your brown sugar and cinnamon pretzels have a **sweet** taste. What taste do most pretzels have?

● If you had a choice among pretzels, potato chips, or popcorn for a snack, which one would you choose?

LIGHTNING BOLT!

Pretzels were first made in Germany many years ago by monks. They were given to children as a reward for learning their prayers. The pretzel twist that we all are familiar with was created to look like the crossed arms of a child praying.

UNBIRTHDAY PARTY

Why wait until your birthday to have a party?

1 Before your party ask a grown-up to help you bake cupcakes. Leave them unfrosted.

2 Your unbirthday party can be as small as two people. You and a friend can decide what the party will celebrate. You might choose to celebrate nature.

3 Make your party hats by making a cone out of a large piece of construction paper. Ask a grown-up to round off the end and staple or tape the hat together. Add a yarn strap and hat decorations that go with your theme.

4 Draw a big picture of your theme for a game of Pin-the-Tail-On. At a nature celebration, you might draw a picture of a big tree with lots of branches and then pin leaves on it.

5 With a grown-up's help, frost the cupcakes and decorate them with sprinkles, chocolate chips, and raisins. Then, in the best party tradition — eat them!

HERE'S WHAT YOU NEED

Construction paper

Yarn

Crayons

ALL ABOUT ME

You may think you know everything there is to know about yourself. After all, you spend more time with you than any one else! Everyone is changing all the time — changing their minds, changing what they like and dislike, or changing how they appear. Here are some fun things to do to find out all about you — as you are today!

GIANT PAPER PERSON

How would you like a giant paper person that looks just like you to hang in your room or on your door?

HERE'S WHAT YOU NEED

| A partner |
| A roll of paper, 36 inches (90 cm) wide |
| Crayons |
| Scissors |

HERE'S WHAT YOU DO

1 Ask someone to help you roll out the paper to a length longer than your height.

2 Lie down on the paper. Ask your partner to trace around your body on the paper with a crayon.

3 Cut out your body shape with the scissors. Color your life-size person wearing your favorite clothes! If you want, you can add yarn for hair and other decorations.

LET IT POUR!

● Double the paper before you cut it. Then staple both cutouts together leaving a small opening to stuff with crumpled newspaper for a three-dimensional paper person.

● Make a shadow drawing by taping a large sheet of white paper on a wall. Place a light in front of the object or person you want to draw. Trace the shadow with a crayon.

● Make photo puppets of your family or friends: Ask a grown-up to help you cut out the faces of family members from some extra photos. Glue the faces to the tops of Popsicle sticks. Make clothes for your puppet out of construction paper and glue them to the stick. Arms can be made from pipe cleaners. Put on a puppet show about your family or friends.

LIGHTNING BOLT!

People come in all different shapes and sizes. Sometimes people wish they could be shaped like someone else, but the truth is there are good things about being just the way you are. The most important reason is that you are the only person in the whole world who looks exactly like you. People love you for being you!

MY FRIENDSHIP TREE

Here's some fun, just wait and see, when you create a friendship tree!

Large piece of oak tag or poster board

Markers

Construction paper

Scissors

Craft glue

HERE'S WHAT YOU DO

1 Ask a grown-up to help you draw a large tree with lots of branches — but no leaves — on your poster board.

2 Draw leaf shapes on the construction paper and cut them out.

3 Make leaves for all your friends by drawing a picture of something they like to do and then, with a grown-up's help, writing their names, one on each leaf.

4 Who should you include? Maybe all the people in your class, or all the people who live on your street, or all the people who live in your house. Your leaves can be for people you know or people you would like to get to know.

- Make a tree for your family or the people you live with. Along with parents, grandparents, sisters and brothers, don't forget to include your pets!

- Play a Friendship Tree game. Ask everyone to think of something funny that happened to them. Share your stories. Which was the silliest?

- Ask your older friends or family members to tell you about their favorite toys and games when they were your age.

Friendship Tree

LIGHTNING BOLT!

Sometimes we feel that we have a whole lot of friends and sometimes we feel that we don't have any friends. There are lots of ways to become someone's friend. You can play with them, share with them, help them with a chore, wait for them when they are busy, listen to them, and laugh with them. And friends don't have to be people — your pets and favorite books can be your friends, too.

EXPLORING ME

Here's a new way to look at yourself — without mirrors.

1 Pretend there are no mirrors. Ask a grown-up to sit in front of you and let your hands tell you about your face.

2 Place one hand on your face and one hand on the grown-up's face. Gently touch the grown-up's chin, then touch your own. Do they feel **alike**? How are they **different**?

3 Touch the grown-up's nose, then touch your nose. Are they the same or different? Continue exploring your face by comparing ears, eyebrows, and lips.

Me

LET IT POUR!

● Without looking in a mirror, draw a picture of yourself. Look in a mirror and compare what you see with what you remembered. Are you happy in your picture? What are the clues that you are happy or sad?

● Look at the pictures in *A Child's Book of Art* selected by Lucy Micklethwait. Are there any pictures of people? What did the artist tell you about people in the picture?

● If there were no mirrors, what are some ways that you might still be able to see your reflection?

MY FAVORITES

Here's a chance to think about your favorites — people, things, thoughts, experiences — and put them all together in a book that you can save forever and ever.

HERE'S WHAT YOU NEED

Paper

Crayons

Stapler or yarn

1 Everyone has different ideas about what is special, or favorite, to them. It could be the sound of your kitty purring on your bed, a special card that is fuzzy on the outside, or a toy you have had a long time.

2 Think about your favorites. Do you have a favorite pet, toy, food, color, or season? How about a favorite friend or grown-up? Talk about what makes each favorite thing or person so special to you.

3 Draw pictures of your favorites on separate pieces of paper.

4 Ask a grown-up to staple your pages together or tie them together with yarn so you will have a book of favorites. What would you like to put on the cover of your book?

LET IT POUR!

● Can you guess someone else's favorites — like their favorite foods, or stories, or baseball cap? What are the clues that help you make a good guess?

● What are your least favorite things? What food or color don't you like? Why don't you like them?

● Try something new a few times. How does it rate on your "favorite meter"? It just might become a favorite after all.

HANDS and FEET

We use our hands and feet for so many things. Take a closer look at both.

HERE'S WHAT YOU NEED

Paper

Crayons

Ruler (measuring stick)

LET iT POUR!

● Count all the fingers on one hand and then all the toes on one foot. How many fingers do you have in all? How many toes?

HERE'S WHAT YOU DO

1 Trace your bare foot on the paper with a crayon. Trace a grown-up's foot also.

2 Ask a grown-up to help you measure the two footprints with your ruler. Which one is bigger? Do you think you could fit your footprint inside of theirs?

3 Next, trace your hands. What is the **same** and what is **different** about your hands and feet?

4 Ask a grown-up if you can try on his or her shoes. What are the things that you notice about wearing big shoes? Now, try on a pair of grown-up gloves or mittens.

COLORS and SHAPES

When you look around, there are so many wonderful colors and unusual shapes everywhere. There are tangerine orange and midnight blue, plus circles, diamonds, and hearts just for you!

MIXING IT UP!

Rainy days are often gray days because the sun isn't shining brightly. There are lots of ways to brighten a gray day including creating your own colors.

HERE'S WHAT YOU NEED

Finger paints

Paper

Popsicle sticks

HERE'S WHAT YOU DO

1 Using a Popsicle stick, scoop out some yellow finger paint in a small circle on the paper. Then, with a clean Popsicle stick, scoop out some blue finger paint on the other side of the paper.

2 Now, take a little yellow and a little blue and mix them together in a new circle. What color did you make?

3 Take a fresh piece of paper, and do the same thing only this time begin with a circle of yellow again and a circle of red. What color did you make? What color did they make?

4 If you paint a picture with these colors you will have blue, yellow, green, red, and orange paints to use.

LET IT POUR!

● Ask a grown-up to cut up a sponge into different shapes. Use the sponge shapes to stamp on your paper with your new paint colors.

● Explore the different colors around your house or classroom. Open up a closet and see how many different colors you can count.

CUT A SPONGE INTO SHAPES

LIGHTNING BOLT!

If you look around you — right this very minute — how many colors do you see? Five? Ten? There are actually hundreds of different colors — just look in a Crayola™ crayon box! You may be very surprised to learn that all these colors actually begin with the three basic colors that you used in Mixing It Up! — red, yellow, and blue.

RAINBOW MOBILE

A rainbow after a summer shower is always a wonderful sight. Here's a way to have a rainbow to brighten every day.

HERE'S WHAT YOU NEED

Construction paper
(rainbow colors)

Safety scissors

Ruler

Clothes hanger

Yarn or string

Crayons

HERE'S WHAT YOU DO

1 Draw a big circle, square, triangle, and a diamond on different-colored pieces of construction paper.

2 Ask a grown-up to help you cut them out and poke a hole in the top of each one. Create your mobile by pulling the yarn through the hole and tying the shapes onto the hanger so they dangle.

3 Draw a huge rainbow arc on a large piece of white paper. Color it with bands of colors. Ask a grown-up to cut it out and hang it from your mobile.

● Cut out a squiggle from construction paper, by cutting a circular snake pattern (beginning on the outside moving inward). Add it to your mobile.

● Here's a way to make a double-decker rainbow mobile. Cut out a large rainbow and shapes. Hang your shapes from the ends of the rainbow arc.

LIGHTNING BOLT!

Every rainbow seems to look different depending on where you are standing, how hard it rained, and how brightly the sun is shining through. Actually, all rainbows have the exact same colors in them and the colors are always in the same order. Isn't that a surprise?

PICTURE PERFECT SHAPES

Frame your favorite photo with the shape of your choice for these fun-to-make frames.

LET iT POUR!

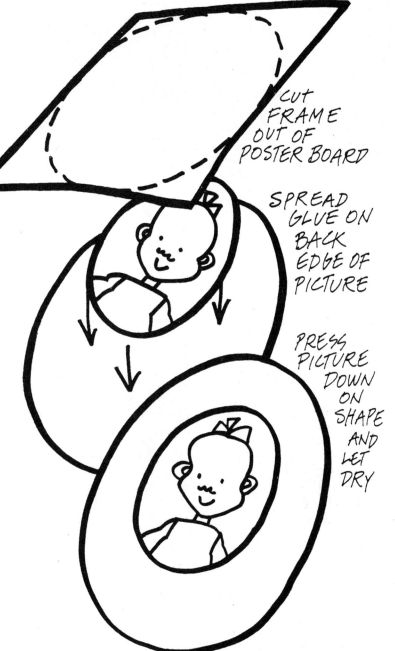

CUT FRAME OUT OF POSTER BOARD

SPREAD GLUE ON BACK EDGE OF PICTURE

PRESS PICTURE DOWN ON SHAPE AND LET DRY

HERE'S WHAT YOU DO

1 Draw some shapes on the poster board. Place the photo on the shape to make sure the shape will fit around the picture.

2 Cut out the shapes with a grown-up's help. Then, place your photo in the middle of the shape so that there is a border all around.

3 Use your finger to apply glue to the border of your picture. Place the photo on the shape again, only this time press down and then let dry.

4 Let dry and hang on a bulletin board or on your bedroom door.

● Attach a magnet, pin, or a folded piece of cardboard to the back for a stand to complete your frame.

● Do a photo sort. Ask if you can have some of the doubles of photos at home. Then make a sorting plan. You can sort by subject (all the pictures of you in one pile, all of your dog in another), by event, by year, or by time of year.

● Begin a personal photo album. Sort your photos (see above) and then carefully glue them onto construction paper. Bind with a yarn tie.

SHAPE MOSAIC

A mosaic is a picture made with little pieces. The pieces can be of anything like bits of tile, tissue paper, tiny pebbles, different colored macaroni. Here you will be using construction paper to make a Shape Mosaic.

Construction paper (assorted colors)

Safety scissors

Craft glue

1 With a grown-up's help, cut out a large triangle from construction paper. Next, using assorted colors of paper, cut out some medium-sized triangles. Then, cut out a bunch of small triangles in different colors.

2 Glue the medium triangles all over the large triangle. Fit as many on as you can. Then, glue lots of small triangles **inside** the medium triangles, placing the small triangles very close together.

3 Now you have a mosaic using three different sizes of triangles.

● Make another Shape Mosaic using large and medium-sized circles, only this time fill the medium-sized circles with buttons glued on for a new kind of mosaic.

● You can make a very pretty mosaic by drawing a huge shape or large flower. Then, paste on small pieces of torn tissue paper.

LIGHTNING BOLT!

When someone asks us to name two or three shapes, most of us will say **circle, square,** and **triangle.** Sometimes we forget that there are many shapes besides those three. Think of the eight-sided shape of a STOP sign, or the four-sided rectangle of a cereal box. Can you think of any other shapes?

TERRIFIC TIE-DYE

All it takes are a few squirts of color, a few twists and ties, and you can make a new shirt that is full of color.

HERE'S WHAT YOU DO

1 Hold your T-shirt or socks with both hands and begin folding and twisting the fabric. Ask a grown-up to help you tie the fabric with string or wrap rubber bands tightly around the fabric.

2 Mix the cold-water dye in the bucket. Fill the empty detergent bottles with the dye. Squirt the colors onto the fabric. (If it's not raining too hard, try this step outside!) Ask a grown-up to follow the directions on the dye to set the colors into the fabric so they won't wash away.

3 Unwrap the tie-dyed shirt or socks and hang up to dry.

1, 2, 3 COUNT WITH ME

You may not know it but you are already counting. Do you sometimes ask for two pieces of candy or three more pushes on the swing? That's what counting is all about — putting numbers to work!

GUESS HOW MANY?

....

When you make a good guess, you think about the question and try to figure out the answer before guessing. Sometimes, though, it is fun to make out-of-this-world guesses!

1 Here is a guessing game that you can play at home, in school, or even in the car. Decide what things you are going to try to Guess How Many? If you are at home, you might guess how many steps go upstairs, how many doors inside the house, how many pots in the cupboard.

2 Draw a picture with some crayons of each thing you are going to guess. Then, make some guesses and put marks for the number you guess next to each picture (six pots would have six lines next to the pot picture).

3 Now, count how many of each thing are really there. With a different-colored crayon, mark how many pots there are. How close were each of your guesses?

● Draw a picture of your house from memory. Then, walk through your house and compare your picture with what you see.

● Count other things in your house like doorknobs, chairs, pictures, and windows. Do you have more windows or doors? Do you have fewer chairs or beds?

● Find out how many eggs are in a dozen.

● Make a Days-of-the-Week bracelet. Take a piece of yarn and on Sunday string on one bead or piece of macaroni. Add one every day until you get to Sunday again. How many beads on your bracelet?

LIGHTNING BOLT!

When people make **wild guesses**, it means they have no idea what the answer is. When people make **thoughtful guesses**, they use clues to get closer to the exact answer. If someone asked you how many glasses of milk you drink a day, you might use the clue "I drink milk at every meal" and then make a thoughtful guess of three.

TICK TOCK, MAKE A CLOCK

There are so many things to like about clocks! Play ones are fun to make, broken ones are fun to take apart, cuckoo clocks are fun to watch, and grandfather clocks are fun to listen to. Best of all, they keep track of the time for us.

HERE'S WHAT YOU NEED

Paper plate

Safety scissors

Cardboard or construction paper

Paper fasteners

Markers

HERE'S WHAT YOU DO

1 Look at a clock. Do you see the numbers 1 through 12?

2 Now, trace over a grown-up's numbers or draw your own numbers on a plate just as they appear on the clock. This is the **face** of the clock.

3 Cut two strips of cardboard for the **hands** of your clock. Make one a little shorter than the other and cut them with pointed ends.

4 Use the paper fastener to attach the hands to the center of the clock face. Now you can move them to show the time.

- Learning to tell time takes a lot of practice. To help you get started, ask a grown-up to set the hands on your home-made clock to a special time, like 6:00 for dinner-time. Now, when you see a real clock with its hands in the same position, you will know it is time for dinner.

- Is there a broken clock or an old watch around your house or classroom? Maybe you can look inside to see all the gears that make the clock go.

- Do you think a clock sound is "tick tock"? What does a clock sound say to you?

LIGHTNING BOLT!

Clocks tell us the time of the day or night. They tell us when to get up in the morning, when to go to school, and when it is bedtime. There are all sorts of different clocks such as **alarm clocks, wrist watches, stop watches, pocket watches, cuckoo clocks, grandfather clocks,** and **clock radios.** Visiting a clock shop can be very noisy if they are all "tick-tocking" at once.

MEASURING MADNESS

Measure by measure this is sure to bring you oodles, gallons, and yards of fun!

HERE'S WHAT YOU DO

1 Look at the different measuring tools. What do you think they would each be best at measuring?

2 Try measuring the cereal with each tool. Which tools work best at measuring cereal?

3 Measure 1 cup (250 ml) of water in the measuring cup. Could you measure the water with a ruler? What does a cup of water weigh?

LET IT POUR!

● No measuring tools? Use your hand or foot to measure. How many hands high is a chair? How many feet wide is the hallway?

● Talk about other measurement tools. What does a clock measure? A thermometer? A calendar? The sun?

● Make up a size measurement and call it a gleeb. How many gleebs long is a pencil? Your foot?

LIGHTNING BOLT!

Ask a grown-up to help you start an "I'm Growing Wall." On the first day of each month, stand straight and tall against the wall. Ask someone to mark with a line where your head touches the wall. Then put the date next to it. Some months you will stay the same and some months you will grow. How much did you grow in a year?

NUMBER DETECTIVE

There are so many numbers hiding throughout your house and classroom. How many can you find?

HERE'S WHAT YOU NEED

Paper

Pencil

Markers

1 Search your house or classroom for numbers! Look at clocks, envelopes, computers, radios, phones, measuring cups — even pencils!

2 Ask a grown-up to write the numbers 1 through 12 nice and large on a piece of paper. You trace over them in markers.

3 Now, be a Number Detective. Every time you see one of those numbers put a check mark next to it.

4 Count up your check marks. Which number did you find most often? Which numbers didn't you find anywhere?

LET IT POUR!

● Practice tracing or writing the numbers 1, 2, 3.

● Celebrate a number each week. If it is "3" week, do everything in three's. Decorate your house with three's. Read three poems at bedtime. Eat your three favorite foods. Put all your pennies in piles of three. Have three crackers for a snack.

● Listen to *One, Two, Three, Count With Me* by Catherine and Laurence Anholt.

ONE, TWO, THREE

Here's a counting game that's as easy as counting 1,2,3!

HERE'S WHAT YOU DO

1 Two players sit face to face and count 1, 2, 3, go!

2 On the word go, both players lower their arms and show one, two, or three fingers. Just as you lower your arms, call out same or different.

3 If both players display the same finger number, then the player that called same is the winner. If the finger numbers are different, then the caller of different wins. If both call the same thing, then no one wins.

LET IT POUR!

● Learn how to count in another language. In Japanese, 1, 2, 3 is *eechee, nee, sahn*. In Italian, 1, 2, 3, is *uno, due, tre*. In Spanish, 1, 2, 3 is *uno, dos, tres*.

● Play Higher-Lower. Call out a number and say higher (or lower). Other person has to answer with an appropriate number.

LIGHTNING BOLT!

Jan-Kem-Po is a Japanese counting game that is played in pairs. (You may know it by Paper-Scissors-Stone.) To play, practice these hand movements first: a closed fist represents stone, a fist with two fingers extended is scissors, an open hand is paper. The two players, hand in the stone position with arm bent at the elbow, say Jan-Kem-Po; on Po the players show either stone, scissors, or paper. The player wins as follows: stone breaks scissors, scissors cut paper, and paper wraps around stone. The ultimate winner wins two out of three rounds.

FLIP!

Most everyone enjoys playing cards. Here's a card game that is good number fun, too.

LET IT POUR!

• Play the same game with the lowest card winning the hand.

• Play Before and After Dominoes. For example, if a three is showing, instead of matching a three, the player can put down a two or a four.

HERE'S WHAT YOU NEED

Playing cards

Partner(s)

HERE'S WHAT YOU DO

1 Remove all the picture cards from deck and place aside. Deal the same number of cards to everyone from the remaining cards.

2 Someone calls out flip and everyone turns over a card. The player who has the highest card wins the round and collects all the cards. If there is a tie, split the cards evenly.

3 When all the cards are gone, the player with the most cards wins.

FUN and GAMES

Everyone's idea of fun is different. You may enjoy running in the wind or splashing in a puddle. Or, at another time, a good game of tag or musical chairs may be just the thing!

ALL-OF-A-KIND

This old favorite is a great way to have fun on a rainy day! You can play with one partner or a lot of partners — or challenge yourself to a game.

ALL·OF·A·KIND

RED

PAT·PAT

HERE'S WHAT YOU DO

1 Sit in a circle or with a partner. Set a slow beat by patting the floor with your hands.

2 Start off the game by saying "All-of-a-Kind" to the two sets of two beats, "such as" to the next two. Then, someone picks a **category**, or kind, of thing, such as colors, shapes, animals, or letters.

> All-of-: (2 beats)
> a-kind: (2 beats)
> such as: (2 beats)
> col-ors: (2 beats)
> gre-en (2 beats)
> re-ed (2 beats)
> pur-ple (2 beats)

3 As you go around the circle, each player must say something from that category in the next two beats. When someone gets stumped, change categories and begin again.

LET IT POUR!

● Pair up and play the same game, but instead of naming all-of-a-kind, say opposites. If the first player says "up," the second player would say "down."

● Play with a partner but instead of taking turns, one partner says all the things in one category and the other counts how many are named. Then, switch roles with a new category.

TAP . TAP

DOWNPOUR

Here's a perfect way to spend a rainy day with your friends!

HERE'S WHAT YOU DO

1 Sit in a circle on the floor. Choose a sound — like rain falling. The first person begins as if the rain is starting to fall (by rubbing thumbs and fingers together), the next will be slightly louder (rubbing palms together), the next might pat hands on knees very quickly, all the way around the circle to the loudest tapping feet faster and faster for a downpour.

2 What other sounds might you build to a roar and then bring back to a purr?

LET iT POUR!

● "Rain, rain go away, come again another day." Begin with a downpour. Then, eliminate each sound until the person rubbing thumbs against fingers is the only sound left.

● Talk about the different ways rain sounds when falling on a tin roof, on a window, or on the car.

LIGHTNING BOLT!

You can make raindrops indoors. Ask a grown-up to boil water in a tea kettle. When the steam begins to rise from the kettle, ask the grown-up to hold a tray of ice cubes above the releasing steam. Watch as tiny water droplets collect on the ice tray where the air is cool. When a few droplets combine and fall you've seen a raindrop!

PLAYING OPOSSUM

When an opossum is frightened or in danger, it "freezes" and doesn't move a muscle. Can you do the same when the music stops?

HERE'S WHAT YOU NEED

Music

Plenty of room to move

HERE'S WHAT YOU DO

1 Have a grown-up turn on the music.

2 Move and dance around the room while the music is playing. When the music stops — FREEZE! Then, begin moving again when the music starts.

LET IT POUR!

● Want to make Opossum even more difficult? Stand on one foot when the music stops.

● Here's a way to make cleaning up a game. See how many toys you can put away while the music is playing. When the music stops, you have to stop!

LIGHTNING BOLT!

Do you know why this game is called Playing Opossum? The opossum is an animal found throughout North America. When it is in danger it first shows its teeth (it has 50!), then it tries to run away. If another animal catches it, it stays absolutely still as if it were dead. Sometimes the animal chasing it will then lose interest and the opossum will get away.

BUG HUNT

There are many bugs that live outdoors, but do you know how many live indoors, too?

HERE'S WHAT YOU DO

1 If you were a bug, where would you choose to live inside? Have you ever seen a spider living in a corner? Or a ladybug near a window?

2 Take out your hand lens and go on an indoor bug safari. What types of bugs do you find? Are they all alive? What do you think they eat?

LET IT POUR!

- You won't find any colorful butterflies inside your house, but you may see a moth or two flying around a light bulb. What is the **same** about moths and butterflies, and what is **different**?

- Play Sofa Search. Pull up the couch cushions and see what you find. Put everything in piles, like Dad's stuff, toys, coins, and pencils. There are quite a few treasures in there!

LIGHTNING BOLT!

Some bugs are good to have indoors. A few spiders help keep down the bug population. When you find pesky bugs indoors, be sure to use a safe, natural remedy to discourage them. Here's one you can do: If you see lots of ants indoors, bring a cucumber to the rescue! Peel a cucumber with a carrot peeler, place the fresh peels around where you see the ants, and the ants will "hit the road."

RIDE THE RAILS

Hop aboard and ride to faraway places on your own imaginary train.

HERE'S WHAT YOU NEED

Chairs (at least 3)

Poster board or butcher paper

Markers

CHOO · CHOO · CHOO · CHOO

HERE'S WHAT YOU DO

1 Set up the chairs in a line so that they look like a train.

2 Draw pictures on the poster board or paper to look like views that you might see from a train. Is your train passing through a city or the countryside? Do you see fields with cows or lots of tall buildings and cars? Is the sun out or is it a cloudy day?

3 Place your drawings outside of your train. Make tickets for your passengers. Sit in your train and pretend you are the train engineer, the conductor taking the tickets, a passenger, or bringing up the rear in the caboose.

4 Does your train have a whistle to blow as you come into the station?

LET IT POUR!

● Have you ever gone for a train ride? If you say the words "clickety-clack, clickety-clack," you will be making the sound of the train's wheels on the track.

● How many different ways to travel can you name? Which ones have you taken a ride on and which ones would you like to go on?

● If you were taking a train ride in another part of the world, what do you imagine you would see out the window?

● Listen to *The Polar Express* by Chris Van Allsburg, about a magical train ride to the North Pole!

NO PEEKING!

This game is fun no matter where you play it — home, school, or car!

HERE'S WHAT YOU DO

1 Ask a grown-up to place some things into the pillowcase, like a spoon, ball, apple, doll, toy car, and book.

2 Tie the bandanna around your eyes to blindfold yourself — or close your eyes.

3 Reach into the bag and take out an object. Feel the object carefully. With your eyes covered, can you tell what the object is? Try the game with different objects.

LET IT POUR!

● When you reach in to touch things, let your fingers tell you the shape of each object and how it feels against your skin. Is it **smooth, bumpy,** or **rough.** These are all helpful guessing clues.

● Try using other senses to play the game. Can you identify items by smell? Can you identify the sounds around your house?

LIGHTNING BOLT!

When you reach into the bag, you are using your sense of touch to help you identify the object. You have five senses in all: touch, taste, smell, sight, hearing. When you use them all, you discover a lot about what is happening around you.

HANDY HELPERS

Put on an apron or some work clothes and become a handy helper!

Dust rag or feather duster

Newspaper

Water and vinegar

Spray bottle

HERE'S WHAT YOU DO

1 You can help a lot on a rainy day. Ask a grown-up to spray a mixture of vinegar and water on the low windows. Crumple up an old newspaper and wipe the windows. By the time you are finished the sunlight might be sparkling through!

2 With a feather duster or light dust rag, carefully dust the legs of chairs, desks, tables, and table-tops. In school, perhaps you can clean the board or help stack some books.

LET IT POUR!

● Do you have any regular tasks to do around your house like make your bed, set the table, hang up your clothes? What do you like to do best?

● What are the Handy Helpers that you can do on a sunny day outdoors?

LIGHTNING BOLT!

Helping around your house or school can be lots of fun — and you are doing something nice for someone else at the same time. There are lots of things you can do to help people and pets: say "hello" whenever you see them, pick up after yourself, bring the newspaper indoors, make a picture to surprise someone, help put the groceries away, or play with your dog or cat.

SKITTLEBOARD

Do you like to play board games? In Skittleboard, you make the board and then have fun playing, too.

HERE'S WHAT YOU NEED

Shirt gift box

Markers or crayons

Ruler

Skittle (button, bottle cap, or small stone)

Partner

HERE'S WHAT YOU DO

1 Take the top or bottom portion of the shirt box and tear off one of the shorter ends. Use a marker to draw a large U in the box, with open end of the U at the open end of the box.

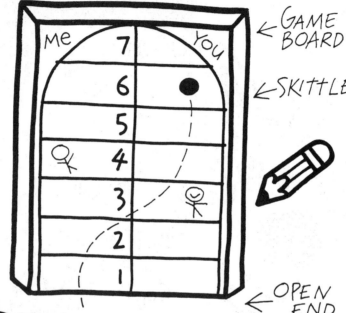

← GAME BOARD

← SKITTLE

← OPEN END

2 Starting at the open end, draw 7 lines across the box. Each line should be about 3 inches (7.5 cm) apart. Draw a line down the center of game board

3 Number each of the center sections 1 through 7, starting at the open-ended side. Now your game board is ready!

Game Plan!

1 This game is for two players. Each player must pick one side of the board. Take turns gently shooting your skittle from the open end onto the game board. Try to land the skittle in one of the numbered squares.

2 When you land your skittle in a square, without it touching a horizontal line, you then can draw on your side of the square a part of a stick figure person. Begin with a head and continue with each landing in that square until you have completely drawn a stick figure person with two eyes, a nose, mouth, two arms, two feet, and a head.

3 Whoever completes a stick figure in a square first, wins.

SIMPLY SCIENCE

Floating eggs? Raising raisins? Invisible art? Could this be magic? It does seem magical, but actually, it is simply science!

RAISING RAISINS

How strong are the bubbles in a soft drink? Stronger than you might think!

Clear drinking glass

Raisins (3)

Club soda or seltzer

HERE'S WHAT YOU DO

1 Fill the glass with club soda. What do the bubbles in the glass do?

2 Drop the raisins into the glass. Did they sink?

3 Now, watch the bubbles and the raisins. What happens to the raisins? Why do you think that happens? What do the bubbles have to do with it?

4 Watch a little longer. What happens next?

LET IT POUR!

● Try the same experiment with a maraschino cherry or a raspberry. What happens?

● Remove the raisins or fruit from the glass. Add a couple squirts of chocolate syrup and a splash of milk. Stir. You made a real New York egg cream! Enjoy.

LIGHTNING BOLT!

The tiny bubbles in soft drinks are filled with gas. This gas is so light that it causes the bubbles to float upwards. When raisins are dropped into the drink, the bubbles stick to the raisins. The light gas then carries the raisins to the surface. When the bubbles reach the surface they burst, and the raisins sink.

CLEAN COINS

When coins are dirty and soap won't do, here's a way to make them look almost new!

HERE'S WHAT YOU NEED

Clear drinking glasses (3)

Vinegar

Baking soda

Cola

Dirty pennies (3)

IN GOD WE TRUST

LIBERTY

1996

HERE'S WHAT YOU DO

1 Place a dirty penny in each of the glasses.

2 In the first glass, pour enough cola to cover the penny. In the second glass, pour about 2 to 3 tablespoons (25-40 ml) of vinegar and about a teaspoon (5 ml) of baking soda. In the last glass, pour enough vinegar to cover the penny.

3 Let the pennies soak for about 3 to 4 hours, then fish them out of the glasses with a spoon. Are all the pennies clean? Which penny is the cleanest?

● Look at each coin carefully. On one side of the coin you will see the year the penny was made. Which of your pennies is the **oldest**? The **newest**? Do any coins show the year you were born?

● Each penny has a **head** and a **tail**. Which side is the head? Toss your penny into the air and guess which side it will land on — heads or tails?

● Save your pennies in a jar. Roll them into coin papers; then visit a bank to exchange your pennies for dollars.

GLASS # 1

ENOUGH COLA TO COVER PENNY

GLASS # 2

2-3 TBS. OF VINEGAR AND 1 TSP. BAKING SODA

GLASS # 3

ENOUGH VINEGAR TO COVER PENNY

LIGHTNING BOLT!

A penny is the name of a coin that is used in Great Britain, the United States, Canada, and other countries. In the U.S., the penny is also called a **cent**. You need 100 pennies to equal one dollar.

FLOATING EGG

If you have ever been to the ocean, you know that it is easier to float in the ocean's salty water than it is in a fresh-water lake. Here is a way that you can see just how salt water helps things float.

1 Fill the glass halfway with water.

2 Gently lower the egg gently into the glass. Does it float?

3 Remove the egg carefully. This time slowly pour salt into the glass of water. What happens to the egg?

LET IT POUR!

● Use a glass filled with salty water and one filled with fresh water. What small items will float in both glasses? What will float only in the salty water? What will not float in either glass?

LIGHTNING BOLT!

Watch a real stand-up egg. Place a tablespoon (15 ml) of salt on a table. Stand up the egg in the salt. Now, gently blow the salt away. What does the egg do?

The egg remains standing because there are still a few grains of salt under the egg that are still working to hold up the egg.

BUBBLE FUN

Bubble here and bubble there.
Bubbles, bubbles everywhere!

HERE'S WHAT YOU NEED

Dishwashing liquid

Water

Cup

Paper clips (2)

HERE'S WHAT YOU DO

1 Ask a grown-up to bend one paper clip to form a circle and the other to form a handle.

2 Mix three spoons of dishwashing liquid into the cup with about a half cup of water.

3 Dip the loop into the mixture and blow steadily through the loop. Watch what happens.

LET IT POUR!

● Pour the bubble formula into a shallow dish. Experiment making bubbles with different objects such as the plastic loops from a six-pack of soda, stencils, etc.

● Sprinkle dusting powder on the surface of a bowl of water. Add a drop of dishwashing detergent. What happens?

● Take a bubble bath!

LIGHTNING BOLT!

Soap bubbles are formed when the dishwashing liquid stretches around tiny pockets of air that are trapped in the running water.

RUB·A·DUB·DUB

BUBBLES IN MY TUB!

MAGIC ART

Here is a way to make a secret drawing or send a secret message.

LET iT POUR!

HERE'S WHAT YOU NEED

Lemon juice

White paper

Cotton swab

Iron (for grown-up use only)

HERE'S WHAT YOU DO

1 Dip the cotton swab into the lemon juice and use it to draw a picture on your white paper. Let dry.

2 Ask a grown-up to place a warm iron on the picture. What happens when the heat from the iron is applied to the picture?

● Lemon juice is clear, or **invisible**, without the heat. Other colorful berries can be used for drawing, too. Mash some straw-berries or blueberries and draw a berry picture using a cotton swab. Can you see it without the iron's heat?

SEE YOU LATER!

INDEX

Little Hands Books

from **Williamson Publishing**

The following *Little Hands* books for ages 2 to 6 are each 144 pages, fully illustrated, trade paper, 10 x 8, $12.95 US. Please see last page for ordering information.

STOP, LOOK & LISTEN!
Using Your Senses from Head to Toe
by Sarah A. Williamson

Children's Book-of-the-Month Main Selection
THE LITTLE HANDS ART BOOK
Exploring Arts & Crafts with 2- to 6-Year-Olds
by Judy Press

SHAPES, SIZES, & MORE SURPRISES!
A Little Hands Early Learning Book
by Mary Tomczyk

The Little Hands
BIG FUN CRAFT BOOK
Creative Fun for 2- to 6-Year-Olds
by Judy Press

SUNNY DAYS & STARRY NIGHTS
A Little Hands Nature Book
by Nancy Fusco Castaldo

Williamson **Kids Can! Books**

The following *Kids Can!* books for ages 4 to 10 are each 160-176 pages, fully illustrated, trade paper, 11 x 8 1/2, $12.95 US.

Winner of the Oppenheim Toy Portfolio Best Book Award!
American Bookseller Pick of the Lists
THE KIDS' SCIENCE BOOK
Creative Experiences for Hands-On Fun
by Robert Hirschfeld and Nancy White

CUT-PAPER PLAY!
Dazzling Creations from Construction Paper
by Sandi Henry

KIDS COOK!
Fabulous Food for the Whole Family
by Sarah Williamson and Zachary Williamson

SUPER SCIENCE CONCOCTIONS
50 Mysterious Mixtures for Fabulous Fun
by Jill Frankel Hauser

Winner of the Skipping Stones Multicultural Award
THE KIDS' MULTICULTURAL COOKBOOK
Food & Fun Around the World
by Deanna F. Cook

VROOM! VROOM!
Making 'copters, 'dozers, trucks & more
by Judy Press

KIDS' COMPUTER CREATIONS
Using Your Computer for Art & Craft Fun
by Carol Sabbeth

KIDS GARDEN!
The Anytime, Anyplace Guide to Sowing & Growing Fun
by Avery Hart and Paul Mantell

Parents' Choice Gold Award Winner!
American Bookseller Pick of the Lists
THE KIDS' MULTICULTURAL ART BOOK
Art & Craft Experiences from Around the World
by Alexandra M. Terzian

Parents' Choice Gold Award Winner!
Benjamin Franklin Best Juvenile Nonfiction Award Winner!
KIDS MAKE MUSIC!
Clapping and Tapping from Bach to Rock
by Avery Hart and Paul Mantell

KIDS & WEEKENDS!
Creative Ways to Make Special Days
by Avery Hart and Paul Mantell

American Bookseller Pick of the Lists
KIDS' CRAZY CONCOCTIONS
50 Mysterious Mixtures for Art & Craft Fun
by Jill Frankel Hauser

Learning the Art of
PYROGRAPHY

Burning Images on Wood, Paper, and Leather

Al Chapman

Dedication

To my three girls, Trinka, Chelsi, and Casey Chapman for sacrificing many occasions we could have shared and played together had I not been involved in my own pursuits. For their understanding and love so freely given to me whether I fail or succeed. They are the spice of my life and I am eternally grateful.

Thanks, Girls.

Library of Congress Cataloging-in-Publication Data

Chapman, Al
Learning the art of pyrography: burning images on wood, paper, and leather / Al Chapman
p.   cm. -- (A Schiffer book for woodworkers)
ISBN: 0-88740-729-3
1. Pyrography. I. Title. II. Series.
TT199.8.C48   1995
745.5--dc20   94-43169
CIP

Printed in Hong Kong
ISBN: 0-88740-729-3

We are interested in hearing from authors with book ideas on related topics.

Published by Schiffer Publishing Ltd.
77 Lower Valley Road
Atglen, PA 19310
Please write for a free catalog.
This book may be purchased from the publisher.
Please include $2.95 postage.
Try your bookstore first.

Acknowledgments

My sincerest thanks to Mack Freeman, Tom Waldun, and Charles Gardner for contributing their works for this book to be used as some of the very best examples of pyrography. I also appreciate their patience in seeing it become a reality after such a long wait. Their contributions were invaluable to my efforts and the standards of excellence I wanted to maintain for the book.

To Jimmy McDaniel of Thomaston, GA, who from the very first always said "you can do it, and you should do it" in regards to selling my works and competing as a carver of wild turkeys. There is no way to calculate the value of his pushy confidence in me. Thanks, Jimmy.

To all of you who have invested in me by buying my works, your purchases have continually encouraged and motivated me. The ultimate compliment. Thanks for your confidence.

To Mr. Ron Ransom, well-known Santa-carving author. Thanks ever so much for all your help and advice in bringing this to a conclusion. I am eternally grateful for your generosity of time and expertise.

To the students of my past pyrography seminars. Your enthusiasm for this art form is the reason for this book. Writing directionals for the classes is how it got started. Had I not witnessed first-hand the joys you experienced at finishing your projects, I would not have been so convinced about the need for the book. Your enthusiasm was contagious and just what I needed. Thank you all.

Last but certainly not least, I want to thank Mr. Bob Boyer of Leisure Time Products, Inc., who is to me the grand daddy of the pyrographic art form. He has done so much for this medium and the artists who pursue it. Thank you, Mr. Boyer.

This wild turkey feather is burned on a maple board. I added the black vermiculation with a dye marker. Collection of Mr. Isaac Ashby, Houston, MO.

Foreword

by Ron Ransom

I met Al Chapman at our first Southeastern Woodcarving show several years ago here in Marietta, Georgia.

Al's work stood out from the many excellent carvings there, and I was particularly impressed with the examples of his pyrography.

My main use for a wood burner is to burn my name on my Santas, and occasionally put detail on a beard. Bill Veasey tried to teach me to do feathers in one of his duck carving seminars, but I think he decided my thumbs were too big.

About a year ago Al shared with me the rough draft of this book. I encouraged him to finish it not only for the serious carver, but also for people young and old, who will enjoy the artistic results that will be gained by following his excellent directions.

The photos are clear, and other illustrations give the type of information that even the beginner will find helpful.

Who knows, I may even try another duck.

Ron Ransom,
author of *Santa Carving,*
Angel Carving and Other Favorites,
Carving Santas with Special Interests, and
Santa Patterns from Ron Ransom

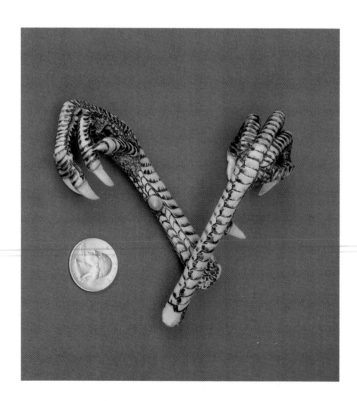

Contents

Introduction

It is not necessary to have a lot of artistic talent to produce beautiful pieces of burnished art. This allows practically anyone who pursues this medium to quickly become proficient at it. Burning patterns in wood or other materials is a gratifying hobby with endless possibilities. It provides an open door for creativity: the techniques may be advanced to produce unbelievable detail and perfection, while even simple techniques can be used to produce beautiful results. Learning pyrography will not require a major investment to get started, since it is quite inexpensive compared to many other hobbies. The uniqueness of the art form produces intriguing and impressive results. I have found most people are fascinated by the process and the results.

I recommend you read a few of the chapters, especially Chapter One, regarding what you will need to get started before you buy your equipment. This is a study book, not just a book of exercises, so you will want to refer to it many times. If by way of this book I have encouraged you with my enthusiasm and taught you with my experience and knowledge, then it has served a good purpose. I am hopeful that one day you will be recognized for your pyrographic art and be able to say this book was a contribution to your success.

A detail of the Court Street chest, showing the variety of techniques I used.

I made this large maple chest, burned with a scene from Court Street, Calhoun, Georgia, as a custom order for Mr. L. C. Stephens (on left). The pattern originated from a postcard postmarked in 1910.

This book is written for both the beginner and advanced pyrography enthusiasts. The exercises and detailed instructions will work for both the simple and advanced burning tools, though it is important to recognize that some of the simpler tools may have limitations with regards to certain techniques and ease of use. Even so, I'm confident this book will serve you well regardless of your level of expertise and will save your countless hours of trial and error.

"Sandy," a pet portrait I burned onto on a wooden plate. Collection of Ms. Trish Cato of Houston, TX.

For this project, I took several photographs of Sandy, and then selected my favorite for the pattern.

SANDY

Chapter One
Innovations and Tools

Many people still have the impression a woodburning tool is nothing more than an old soldering iron with a sharp point. This was more the truth a few decades back, but over the past twenty years, some marvelous innovations have come to be, thanks largely in part to woodcarvers who were trying to achieve more lifelike detail in their carvings. Available are several different burning systems with temperature controls, which will accommodate a wide variety of differently shaped tips. Like most everything else, some have certain advantages or features over others which you may or may not desire. Like most art mediums, the tools you choose to use can have a great effect on your level of achievement and the quality of your work. There are people who can do wonders with the simplest of tools, while others find the more advanced tools necessary. The more serious artisans will usually advance to a level where the need for a better or faster tool becomes evident and necessary. What

you want to achieve, your particular style and technique, along with your commitment to the effort are all factors in determining which tools are best suited for you. My advice is, if you can afford one of the more advanced systems, start with it because it will usually offer more versatility and be easier to use. However, if your budget is a factor, a simpler and less expensive burning tool will suffice—just keep in mind it's limitations regarding things such as life-like detailing and difficulty of use.

I don't want you to be discouraged if you are trying to do something your tool is not best designed for. Most woodburning systems offer a variety of interchangeable tips which will serve most if not all of your purposes. You can, however, produce marvelous results with only a few of the differently shaped tips by learning some of the techniques found in this book.

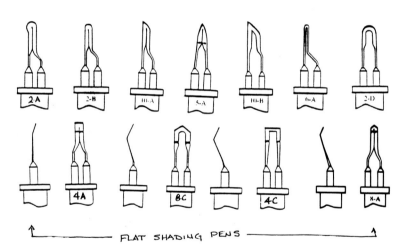

A variety of flat-edge and shading pen tips offered by Detail Master.

A few of the Colwood tips available.

Again, you will know and discover what suits your needs best as you experiment and try new and different things. It all depends on what you want to accomplish and produce when selecting your pens. What works best for you will not necessarily work well for someone else. Most are designed with certain purposes in mind, and some manufacturers offer custom shapes upon request. For those of you who are interested in flat art only, there will be tips designed for the carver that you will not need.

The best advice I can give you is to read the manufacturers' suggested uses to see what will be most advantageous to you. I have found there are three or four shapes I use more often than others, only because they suit my style of burning. You will most likely discover a few that are your primary tips which suit your needs as well. Don't be overwhelmed or confused by the selection. Your burning system will more than likely come with a variety of tips. One tip in particular I like because of it's versatility is the spear shaped tip which has two sharp sides. I recommend this as your first choice when adding to your collection because it works well for both flat art and carving artists.

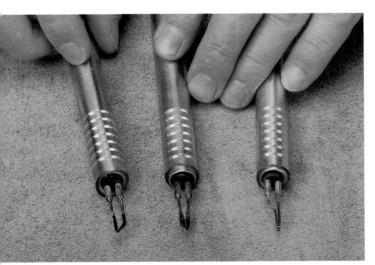

Three favorite tips—1-C, 5-A, and 6-A—from Detail Master Pens.

Follow the manufacturer's advice on sharpening and caring for your pens. For ultra fine detail, you must keep them sharp. This requires little effort and the rewards will be evident in your work.

Remove char build-up from your tips with sanding paper no coarser than 200 grit.

Repeat as necessary.

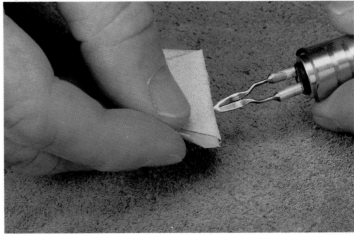

Once the tip is clean, you may need to hone the edges.

These two designs were made with the same type of pen tip, on the same temperature setting. The one on the left was done with a properly sharpened tip, while the one on the left was done with a dull tip. The differences are obvious.

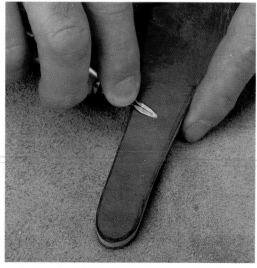

Use a very fine grit stone, and lightly stroke the tip, to hone the edges.

A few strokes on a leather strop will finish the job.

Notice how sharply beveled the edge is.

Chapter Two
Getting Started

Much depends on what you have in mind of doing with your woodburner. For most purposes such as flat art and detailing simple carvings, a burning system with a couple of tips is all you will need. In addition to your burning system, you will need material to burn your patterns on and a few patterns or ideas. If you are a beginner, I suggest you start with practicing on small pieces of 1/4" finished plywood such as birch, ash, maple, or some other fine grain wood. A 4' x 8' sheet which can be purchased from your local building supply will go a long way. If you can find 1/2 or 1/4th of a sheet, this will be enough. You will need to cut this into smaller workable pieces. You may want to start out on small basswood plaques, or rounds (pieces cut diagonally to the grain). There are many premade but unfinished pieces such as "what-not shelves," towel and spice racks, etc., which are made from pine. Although pine is not ideal for scenic plaques and is not my first choice of wood, you can decorate these pieces with remarkable results with your burner. They are not expensive and can be decorated to personalize them. You may want to use your burning pen to outline a pattern to be painted. It makes painting a lot easier and you can create textures without painting them in.

Basswood plaques like these provide a good working surface, and can be found in most arts and crafts stores.

Use practice boards to get familiar with the types of lines and textures you can burn.

Don't confine yourself to just flat art pieces on wood. You can use your burning system on many different objects and materials, some of which will be covered in the following chapters.

How you plan to finish your project and the subject matter involved will dictate what type of wood is best suited for a particular piece.

Ideally, avoid woods such as pine which have hard and soft areas. Use a wood with a less distinctive grain which will not detract from the burned images and allow for consistent burning. If you are going to stain the piece, use the harder type woods such as clear maple which are light in color and absorb less stain. A note of warning: make sure your workpiece is clear of any milling or sanding marks before you burn your pattern. Once stained, any tell-tale scratch or mark will be very evident. You may have to sand it off, taking much of your burning with it, if you failed to check it thoroughly. This has happened to me more often than I care to admit. Don't shortcut your preparations by getting overly anxious; it will only cost you more time and effort.

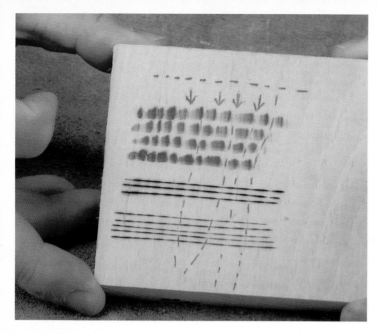

As illustrated in this pine board, hard and soft veins in the grain can disrupt burning. Note how these continuous strokes are broken up by the grain.

When I stain a project, I prefer to use Red Devil wood stain, and I use their #40 Cherry a lot. Their stain has a thick consistency I find easier to work with. The color of the #40 Cherry works well with almost all my projects. For instructions on staining your projects, read Chapter 6.

Different grains and types of hard and soft woods all have different burning qualities.

Mill marks can be project hazards you will want to avoid. It is a must to sand them out if you are going to put a stain finish on the piece. These marks are hard to see on bare wood, but stain will make them very obvious.

Experiment with different woods to see what kind of results you can obtain. There are simply too many variables to cover them all and a lot will depend on your own style of burning. Solid hardwood boards are expensive and wide widths difficult to find. For larger projects, you may want to go with finished plywood. Ash, maple, and birch are readily available at most building supply establishments. You can also find basswood plywood in thin thicknesses at your local hobby shop.

If you are not artistically inclined, you might want to try using some of the transferable patterns available. Your hobby or crafts store should have these as well. There are many books which depict pen and ink illustrations by different artists covering every kind of subject matter. These are especially good for they show you exactly what lines need to be burned to duplicate the illustration. Coloring book patterns are excellent for beginners and youth in honing their skills. Transfer paper will be needed to put them on wood. Use only the graphite type which can be easily erased and not the ink type.

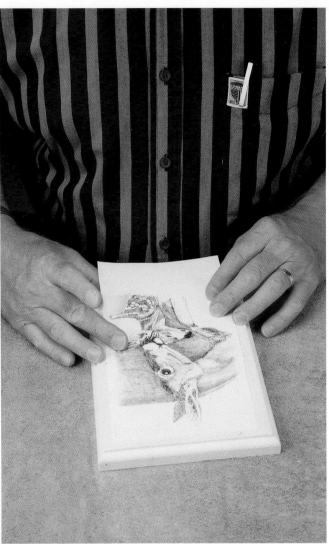

Then tape it down. I tape it only at the top, so that I can lift it to check my progress as I trace.

Once you have your burning pen and piece of wood, you are ready to start. Keep safety in mind before and when you start burning. I suggest these safety rules and guidelines.

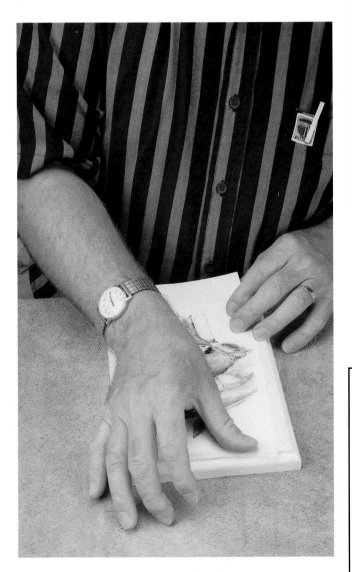

To start, center your pattern onto the plaque,

SAFETY RULES

Never use burner around combustible fuels or gases.
Keep work area neat and orderly.
Make sure paper materials such as your patterns are out of the way.
Do not leave children unsupervised while they are operating a burning system.
Follow instructions and safety precautions for your system.
Always unplug after use.
Store pens with caps covering pointed or sharp edges.

Chapter Three
Practicing Patterns and Strokes

Even if you are already quite proficient at woodburning, you may learn some easier methods by practicing these exercises. Give them a try before moving on to advanced techniques.

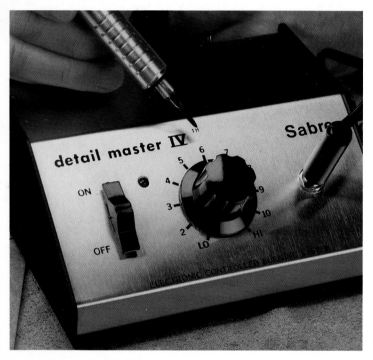

Set your burning system temperature control around the mid-range to start out with.

For general purposes, set the temperature control on your burning system somewhere near the mid-range mark. You may adjust this once you determine several factors. Primarily, the speed at which you work will determine the proper setting, however, the hardness of your wood, the wattage output of your system, the type pen being used, all contribute to proper temperature selection. It's important to remember to work in a draft-free environment, because even a slight draft can effect your consistency in burning. All of this may sound difficult to overcome, but it only takes only a few minutes to resolve.

Before turning on your system to start the first exercise, review the safety tips. Get the feel of the pen in your hand and know how the cord affects it as you move it about. Make a few cold runs before actually attempting to burn these patterns. You may need to rearrange the cord at the back end of the pen to accommodate control of the pen.

Hold the pen just as you would a pencil. Place your hand on your workpiece just as if you were fixing to write a letter. If right handed, roll your hand to the left until the pen points almost directly away from you (just opposite for left handers).

Attempt to find your most comfortable position while maintaining the position of the pen pointing directly away. Don't be discouraged by this awkward position, you can modify it for more comfort by positioning the work piece once you get the feel of things. Now, without lifting or sliding your hand, move the pen tip forward and backwards using your thumb and fingers in what I refer to as the piston motion. By keeping your pinky finger resting on the work surface, either curled under your hand or extended out, your hand will be supported and allow for more accuracy and consistency as you burn. The position of your pinky finger resting, either under or out, is determined by what is most comfortable for you. You might want to try positioning your pen over the actual diagrams in this book, and without touching the paper, move the tip over the lines in a tracing fashion. Once you feel confident, turn your system on and begin with the first exercise.

Always position your workpiece to accommodate for accuracy and comfort. You will need to remind yourself often to do this.

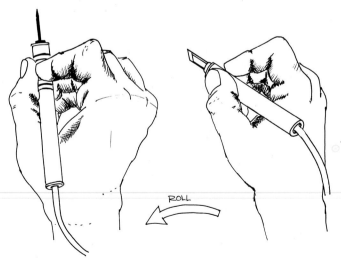

This is the proper way to hold your pen. Note that the shaft (handle) of the pen is in direct alignment with your forearm. The back of the handle should be pointing at your elbow.

HAND POSITION

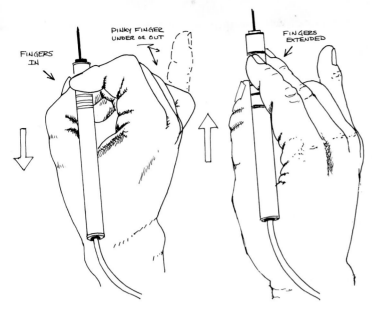

THE 'PISTON METHOD'

EXERCISE #1
STRAIGHT LINES

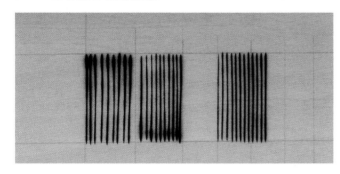

The left and center exercises show the results of an inconsistent burn. Dark at the top indicates a slow start; dark at the bottom indicates a pause at the finish. Practice until you can achieve a burn that looks like the one at the right.

This exercise will teach you how to be consistent and accurate. This technique is used in many ways to detail bird feathers, duplicate hair, and as you will learn later, create depth in your subject mater. Start at the top of each line and pull the pen tip toward you using the piston method. Don't be overly concerned about the length just now. You will discover with your first few attempts if you need to slow down, speed up, or raise or lower the tip temperature. I strongly suggest going slow at first. Your speed will come naturally and you can raise the temperature as you progress. Your main concern at this point is getting the feel of things and trying to achieve consistency in the burn. If your lines are burned darker at the top, it's because this is the point and time when your tip is hottest, and much of the temperature is lost when it initially touches the wood. The trick

to overcoming this is to have the pen in motion as it touches the wood and adjust your speed accordingly to maintain a consistent burn depth and darkness. Pressure should only be slight and added pressure should never be used as a means to achieve darker lines.

Unnecessary pressure is rough on your tips and fatiguing to your hand. Continue this exercise several times over, and see how close you can bring the lines together and maintain separation. Not just now, but eventually you should be able to burn 12 distinctive lines per 1/4", which is excellent.

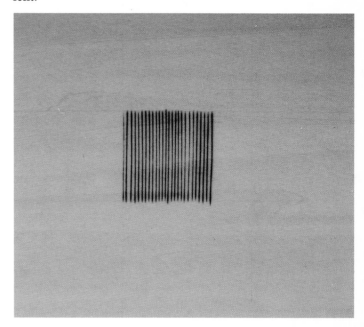

Practice keeping your lines clean, clear and close.

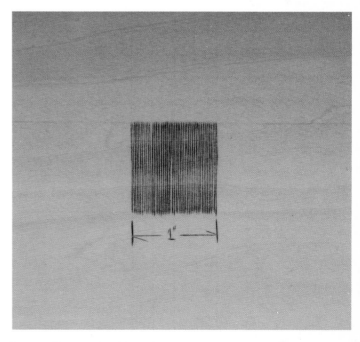

Eventually, you should be able to get as many as 12 lines into just a 1/4" space!

EXERCISE #2
CURVES

This exercise will help you to develop pen tip control and flexibility. To perform this exercise you will need to hold your burning pen at a high angle and rotate it by rolling it in your fingers. Start at the top with the blade of your pen angled in the direction you are proceeding.

As you progress through the curves, roll the pen between your thumb and fingers, keeping the tip blade angled in the direction you need to go. This rotating action works best when you start by holding the pen tip as if you were fixing to burn a straight line as you did in exercise #1. Rotate the pen in your fingers clockwise until the blade angle is aligned in the direction you are to start, maintaining the same thumb/finger contact on the pen handle. As you proceed through the curve, your thumb and finger will return to their original position then pass in the opposite direction as you progress through the curves. When you reach the end of the lines, your fingers should be in the position you started with. If your fingers get too warm from the heat, you can raise your workpiece as if it were a mirror and you are looking into it. This will allow the rising heat from the tip to pass your fingers. This will also help to keep your pen handle from getting too hot.

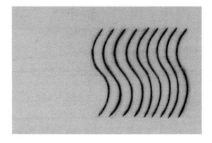

Try to get smooth, evenly spaced curves, with a consistent burn.

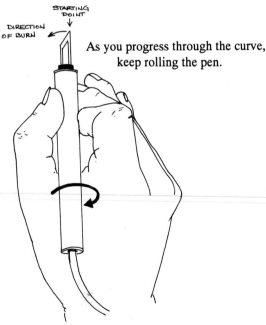

As you progress through the curve, keep rolling the pen.

ROTATION

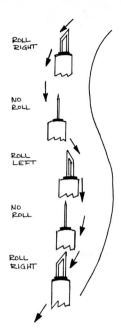

The pen should roll between your finger and thumb so that the tip is always slanted in the direction of the curve.

ANGLE DIRECTION

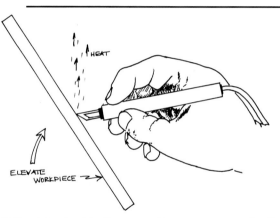

If the rising heat bothers your fingers, you can raise the piece to allow heat to escape.

ELEVATING THE WORKPIECE

EXERCISE #3
CIRCLES

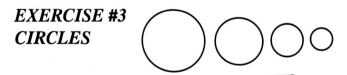

Learning to burn circles will advance your skills remarkably and the techniques I recommend you use will be very advantageous to you in producing your own works. This technique will be especially useful in lettering. For this exercise, try different size circles. Draw circles around a quarter, nickel, penny and dime. Start with the quarter size first, working down to the smallest dime circles. Your burning pen position will work best when it is at a 90 degree angle to the work piece.

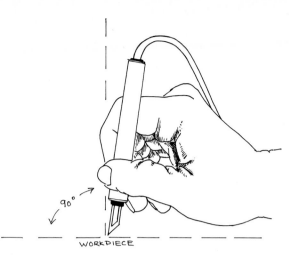

It is best to keep your pen at a 90 degree angle to the workpiece when burning circles.

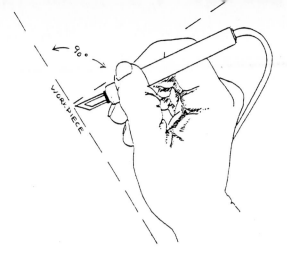

Even if you elevate your workpiece for better visibility and to allow rising heat to bypass your fingers, it is important to maintain the same 90 degree angle.

RIGHT ANGLE POSITION

ELEVATING THE WORKPIECE

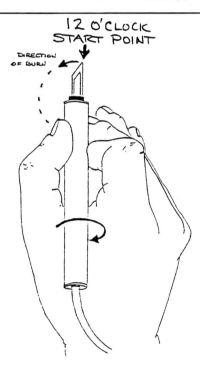

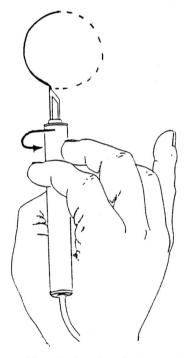

Raising the top edge of the work piece as if you were using it as a mirror to see your face, position the tip of the burner at the 12 o'clock position of your circle. Rotate the pen by rolling your fingers until the blade tip is in a horizontal position.

Start at the top and burn down the left side of circle, allowing your fingers and thumb to rotate the pen so the blade is always angled into the arc. Continue until you reach the bottom. Start again at the top and repeat this same procedure down the right side. Note the rotation is just the opposite for the right side of the circle. You can maintain the pen's rotated position in your hand at the bottom of the left side, move to the top, and start down the right side. This method will improve your uniformity. Continue practicing the circles until you can consistently connect both starting and finishing points while maintaining the roundness.

Note the finger positions for burning circles. Roll to the right to burn left, and roll to the left to burn right.

ROLLING THE PEN

Elevate the top edge of the workpiece so that you are looking directly at the flat plane, and position your pen so that it is at a right angle to the plane. Position the tip of the pen at the 12 o'clock position of your circle. Rotate the pen by rolling your fingers until the blade is in a horizontal position.

EXERCISE #4
CROSSHATCHING

Learning to crosshatch will teach you one way to create shading, texture and depth. This technique is often used with pen and ink drawing and was used extensively a century ago in producing lithographs for printing. A good example of how it can be used to create depth is seen when applied to a circle. You can make a circle look like a three-dimensional ball. You can also add dimension to objects by using this method to illustrate their dark or shady sides. The closer your lines are together, the darker the area becomes. Use your pencil to shade it first by laying the lead flat-ways, or draw in a smaller circle to locate the highlighted spot.. Go over the shaded areas with your burning pen using the crosshatch method. Once complete, lightly sand it, dust it off, and check your progress. You may want to use a soft brass bristle brush to clean out your burns.

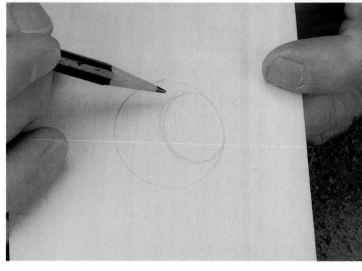

When you begin crosshatching, it is a good idea to pencil in the borders of the light-reflecting areas of the object. These will show you where to stop burning. On this ball, the light will appear to reflect on the smaller circle I have drawn in.

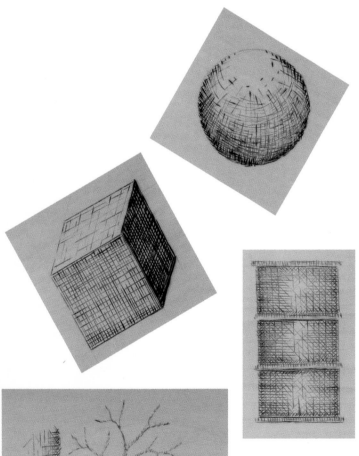

Some examples of crosshatching.

The first step in burning the crosshatch is to cover the shaded area with lines all running parallel, in one direction.

Then go over the same area in the perpendicular direction.

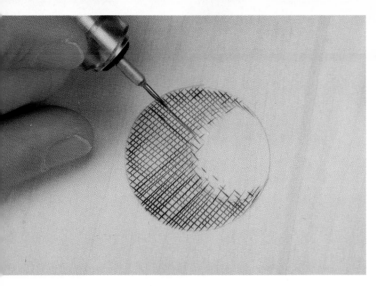

Extend some of the lines into the lighted area, and add some dashes, to soften the shading.

Next go in a diagonal direction, but extend the lines only part way up to your pencil-line curve, to soften the shading even more.

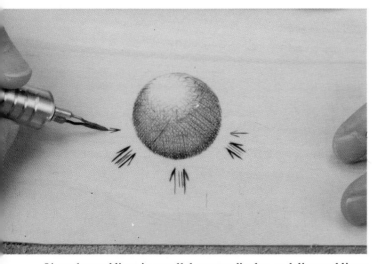

I have burned lines in parallel, perpendicular, and diagonal lines; the last step is to burn lines in the fourth direction, diagonal but perpendicular to the first diagonal, as indicated by this arrow.

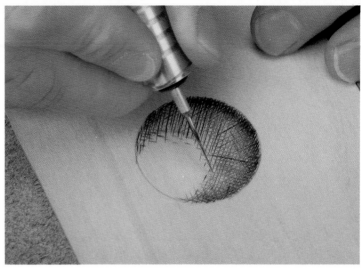

I use sporadic hashmarks wherever needed to pull it all together with a more consistent graduation of tone.

EXERCISE #5
FLAT-EDGE BURNING

This technique is primarily used for shading flat art pieces. However, it can also be applied to carvings to raise areas adjacent to the burn. It is especially good for raising quills of feathers. There are pen tips designed to produce these results, but they can be achieved with most conventional tips that have a flat, straight edge. All that's required is that you lay your pen tip on the surface at a nearly flat angle. It usually requires a much hotter operating temperature. Draw a one inch square on your board and try to get an evenly shaded pattern across the entire square inch. Adjust your temperature so that it burns fairly dark. Experiment with your speed for different degrees of darkness. You will get a much more consistent burn when you stroke the tip with the grain rather than across it. You will find this technique works differently on different types of wood, and sometimes differently on different areas of the same board. You may have to adjust your temperature and/or speed to compensate for these inconsistencies.

The pen tips designed specifically for this type of burning are shaped to allow the pen to be held conventionally. They come in a variety of widths and shapes.

It is possible to use a conventional tip to do flat-edge burning, as illustrated here.
FLAT-EDGE BURNING

19

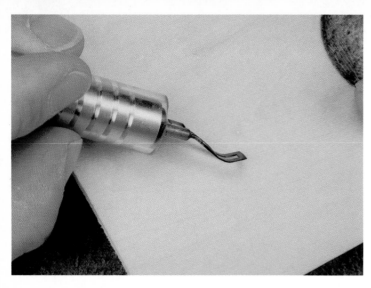

This type of flat-edge pen has a bend in it that allows you to hold it at a more natural angle while you use this technique.

A flat-edge DetailMaster #4-C pen, using the full surface.

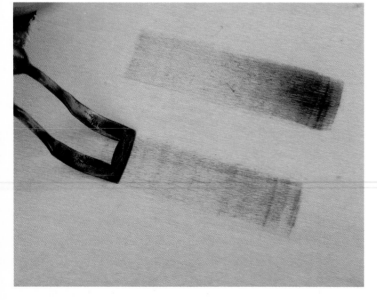

You will need to keep your pen in motion to avoid a dark spot at the beginning of a burn.

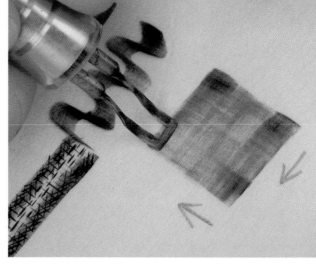

When you are shading with a flat-edge pen, burning over the area a second time in a perpendicular direction creates a more consistent shade. Again, you can see what happens if you don't keep your pen moving at a consistent speed; note the darkness of the burn in the corners.

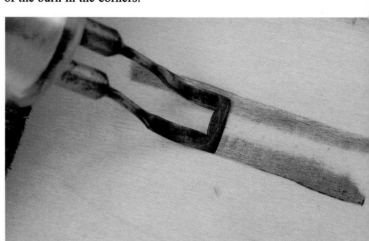

Tilting your pen edge to provide greater pressure first on one side, and then on the other can create a cylindrical look, good for shading tree limbs which can later be detailed.

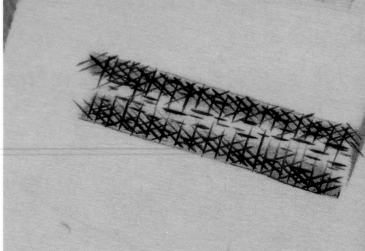

By combining crosshatching with the flat-edge technique, you can create texture. This technique is great for depicting tree limbs.

Here I have chosen to use the straight-edge pen, so that I can do flat-edge burning in some tight curves.

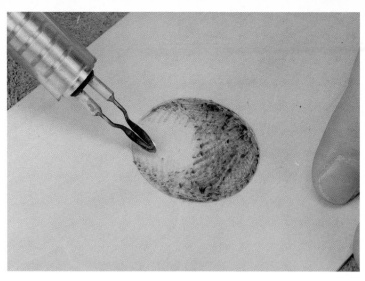

As you do with crosshatching, pull a few light lines into the highlight, to soften the contour.

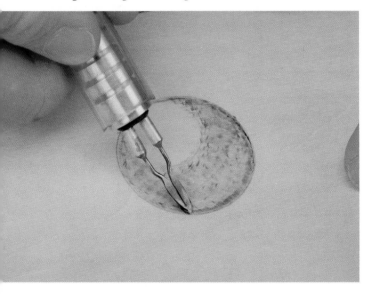

Like I did with crosshatching, I apply one layer of shading over the entire area, except the highlight.

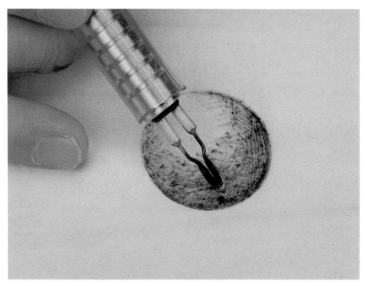

Do another layer of flat-edge shading just along the bottom of the ball, for extra depth. Use a hotter temperature to make the area darker. Afterwards, blend the areas.

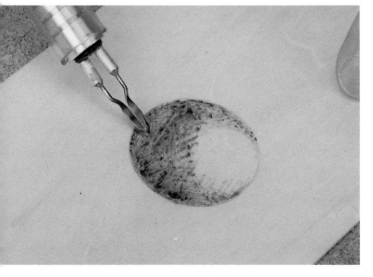

Then I go back over to do a second, darker layer, but do not work all the way up to the highlight.

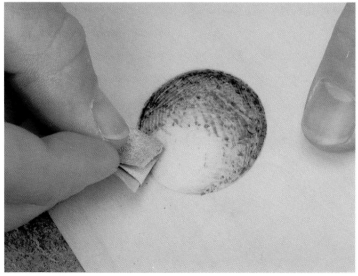

You can soften the edges more by using a fine-grit sandpaper.

EXERCISE #6
STIPPLING

Stippling is the use of dots to create shadows and 3-D effects in images. Some artisans use this technique entirely to create their patterns. It's a time-consuming process, but produces some marvelous results. You will want to use a sharp pointed pen for this exercise. Try to create a three dimensional look of an object by adding more dots to darken the areas where shadows dictate, and gradually reducing them as you proceed to the light-reflecting areas.

The script pen (#6A) manufactured by Leisure Time Products for their Detail Master Systems works well as a stippling pen.

Photographs of Stippled Works
by Thomas Waldun

The woodburnings of a goose and bass by Mr. Thomas Waldun of Hephzibah, Ga. were done entirely by stippling. They are superb examples of this technique and the detail, depth, and three dimensional effect which can be achieved. Note how Tom used heavy concentrations of dots to create the dark areas and only scattered them in the white and light-reflecting areas.

Photographs by Christina Manning of Augusta, Ga.

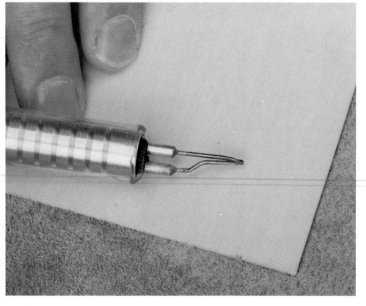

An example of how stippling can make a circle into a ball.

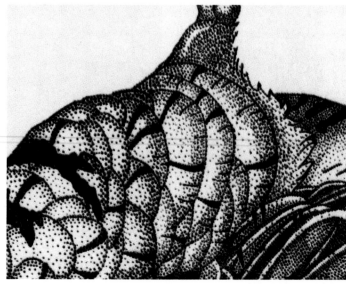

The 6-A pen tip (script pen) from Detail Master.

Another of Tom Waldun's works using stippling. Note the shading inside the mouth of the bass and how Tom created the black pattern down the side of the fish by adding more dots.

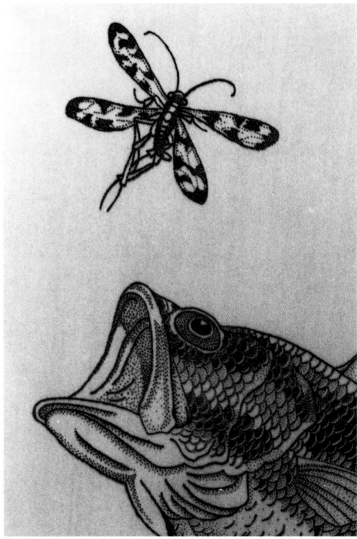

Chapter Four

Creating Your Own Patterns

As noted previously, there are pattern books available which have a wide variety of patterns as well as artists' books with depictions which have few copyright restrictions. Pen and ink drawings are an excellent source for material as they lend themselves perfectly to this medium. Photographs from magazines can be a good source as well: however, a word of caution for you regarding copyrights on photographs and other material. Even if a photograph is not copyrighted, it is considered to be the property of the photographer, magazine, etc., and caution should be used in duplicating it. Use them for reference and study to create a pattern of your own. If you have access to a copy machine, this will help you a great deal, especially if you can enlarge or reduce with it. You can select your subject from several different sources, compose them as you like, and make your pattern on the copy machine. I have often used part of a photograph such as a head, traced it, then drawn in the body or other parts as I wanted them. More likely than not, if you use subject matter from two or more sources, you will have to compare them for proper perspective and enlarge or reduce them for proportions. This can be tricky, but it will work. Also, if you are not too artistically inclined and need some help, almost everyone knows someone who is willing to lend a hand. Usually those talented people are flattered by a request and will gladly assist you in your composition.

Don't forget your camera. Use it to capture an image you want. You can put the photos on a copy machine to enlarge them to desired size. Make a tracing from these using a pencil. Go back over your penciled tracing with a black fine-point ink pen. Use the ink pen in the same fashion as you would your burn tip, applying the crosshatch technique. This will give you a better pattern for your actual work piece, as well as a good idea of what it will look like.

I border the areas that are white so I can be sure not to burn those.

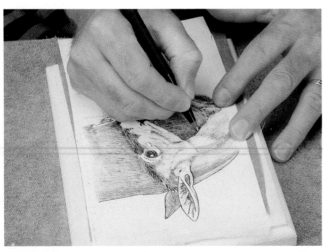

After transfer paper has been placed between the pattern and the workpiece, I use a red ballpoint pen to transfer the pattern. The red pen allows me to see where I have traced.

You can also make use of slides by projecting the image onto paper to the desired size, and then tracing the images with a pencil. Go back over your penciled tracing with pen and ink as mentioned above. An alternative to tracing a pattern onto your workpiece is burning directly through the pattern. This is easily done but you will need to be careful how you go about it to keep it from coming apart. I like to burn from the center of the pattern out to the edges and avoid burns that will separate or fragment the pattern.

My primary concern is burning in the major reference elements of the pattern and filling in the details after the pattern has been removed. You will also want to keep some scotch tape handy to use on areas of the pattern you have burned. Patching these cuts will help keep things in place and keep your pattern from falling apart. This technique is especially useful when burning on leather, paper, and other materials or objects where you want to avoid leaving the tracing paper marks. Also, use it when the surface of your workpiece doesn't take the tracing very well, such as on slick, hard surfaces.

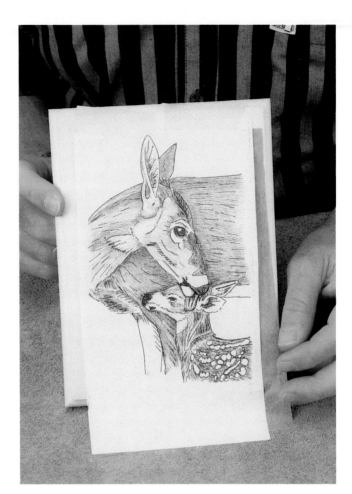

The entire pattern, traced out.

Occasional marks indicating hair direction for guidance.

For pattern resources, I have what is known as a morgue file. In this I keep photo's from magazines on anything which may be of use. I categorize them to aid me in quick reference. If you have a particular subject matter you want to do such as horses, barns or old house scenes, flowers, birds, bears, bunnies, etc., look for publications which will depict these. I enjoy wildlife of all sorts, so I advertised to buy old issues of *National Wildlife Magazines*. I bought several years worth for about ten cents each and cut out all the photos I thought I might have a use for. You can do the same with other subject matters. It won't take long to build a morgue file to supply you with plenty of pattern material.

Along with your morgue file, keep a supply of quality tracing paper handy to aid you in composing your patterns.

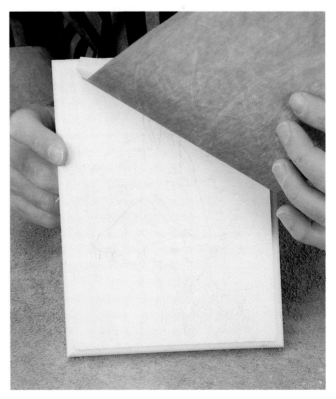

These lines will guide me as I burn the wood.

Instead of using transfer paper to trace the pattern, another technique is burning your guide-lines directly through the paper. However, much caution should be used. You'll need to avoid outlining areas with solid lines.

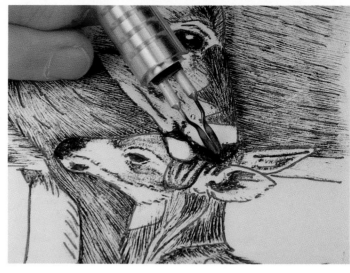

Use the flat of the tip for areas that are not heavily textured...

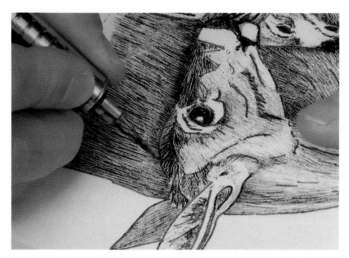

By burning up TO a line, using the hair direction as a guideline, a broken line is created showing the brow and nose of the doe,

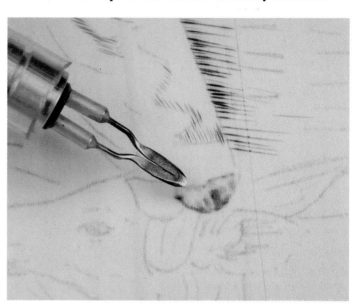

to acheive a softer transfer.

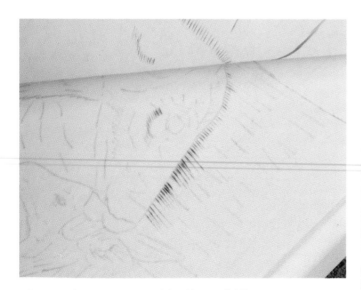

without using any unnatural-looking solid lines.

On outer edges like the ear, I use very short burns for outlining, to avoid creating a solid line. See the next photo for a look at the results.

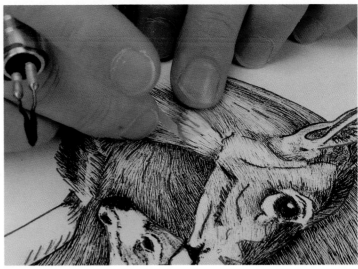

This broken line makes for a much more natural look.

I use scotch tape to hold together sections of the pattern that are coming apart from the burns.

These burn marks will suffice to provide guidance for my woodburning.

Photographs of works by
Charles Gardner

A very good example of using a photograph for pattern purposes is found in this woodburning by Mr. Charles Gardner of Virginia Beach, Va. He used a photograph of his wife to burn this image on a basswood plaque.

Mr. Gardner took up the hobby of woodburning only a few years ago at the age of 67. Nearly all of the works by him pictured in this book were done in the first two years of his new-found interest.

Owl.

Eagle.

Doves.

Martins.

Chapter five
Advanced Techniques

Very often, it's not what you burn so much as what you *don't* burn that counts. Learning what, when and how much to burn is something you will be discovering through experience as long as you continue in this medium. More often than not, I have seen beginners over-burn their pyrographs in their first attempts. The following tips and techniques can save you many hours of work and get you past the many obstacles and hurdles you might have experienced without them. Whenever possible, avoid using burn lines which have a tendency to outline your subjects. This applies more to natural subjects than man-made or architectural ones. There will always be exceptions to this rule, but you will learn from experience when to apply it. Most often, this applies to furry, hairy, fuzzy, and feathery subjects, light-reflecting edges of objects, and objects which are white or light in color. Reflecting light tends to obliterate outlines to your vision; consequently you will want to do this in your burning so it will look more natural and lifelike. In the next chapter, entitled "Finishing Techniques," you will find some tips to aid you in this effort.

You can achieve a much more natural effect if you avoid using solid outlines when you burn your images. See what a difference it makes in the racoon and the feather shown here.

BURNING TO A LINE

There will be occasions when your burn mark extends past a point or line where you intended to stop. This happens frequently when lettering or in depicting corners where it becomes quite obvious. The cause is usually in the heel portion of the burning tip and the problem can be avoided in a couple of ways. First, try holding your pen at a higher angle which reduces the surface contact. If the problem continues, try a more pointed tip in the same fashion.

When lettering, turn your piece upside down, and finish your line by starting at the guide line and connecting it with the original. Taking care to avoid these little mistakes will go a long way in improving your work.

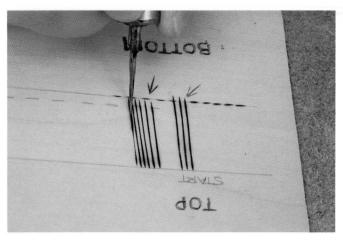

To avoid this, stop a little bit before your bottom line (I have penciled in a second line, to let me know when I am getting close).

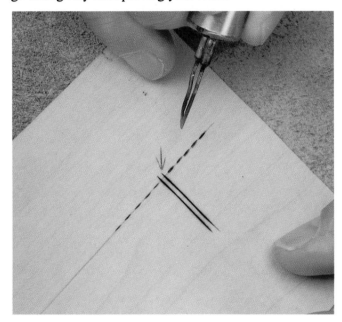

Many pyrographers accidentally over-extend their lines. Here, the tip of the pen stopped on the dashed line, exactly where I wanted the line to end, but when I lift the pen I see that the line itself went too far.

Then turn the piece around, and start with your pen tip at the bottom. Use short burns to connect the bottom with the rest of the lines.

Here you can see why: the heel of the pen went too far.

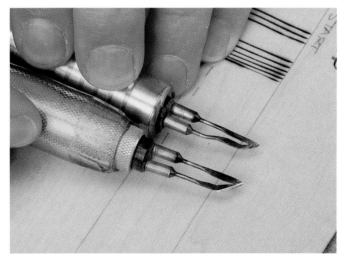

You may find that using a pen with a more acute point minimizes this problem.

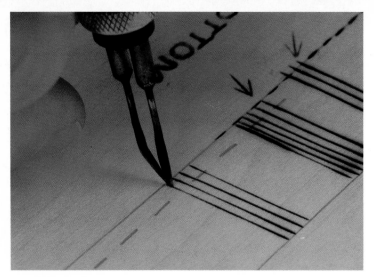

Holding the pen at a higher angle is another way to avoid over-extending the line with the heel.

Fine hair or fur should be approached the same way coarse fur is, with the exception of temperature and depth—don't burn as hot or as deep. Make your strokes comparable and proportionate to the length of the hair or fur you are trying to create. In areas of an animal where the hair or fur makes sharp turns or curves, shorten your burn strokes for a more contoured effect. In areas of white or where light is reflecting, much less burning will be necessary. A more suggestive technique will be the rule. I will explain that method later in the chapter.

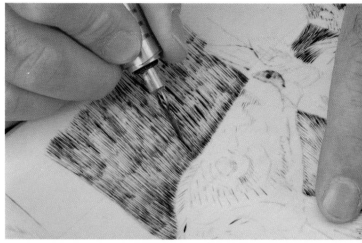

Using your traced or burned pattern guidelines to determine direction, burn in your first layer of fur. The variations in darkness in these burns are caused by the grain, but still it is important that you keep your stroke consistent.

HAIR & FUR

When illustrating hair or fur, the primary consideration is the coarseness. For coarse fur such as on a bear, burning deeper into the wood will usually produce better results. At least two and often three burnings over the same area will often be required.

I have discovered that sanding between burns flattens the tops of the ridges created by the burned fur lines, thus allowing better pen control during the next burn and better detail. With the sharp ridges removed, the edge of your pen tip is less likely to follow the path of a previous burn line. Even with just one burn you can make it look good, but don't stop there. Sand it and do it again. More likely than not, you'll never be satisfied again with just one burn.

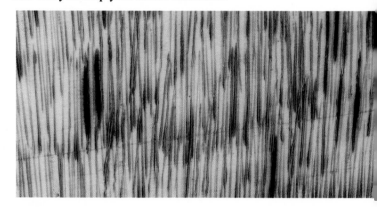

Close-up of the first burn. The darker, heavier lines here were my original guidelines, and as I add more layers of fur they will blend in better.

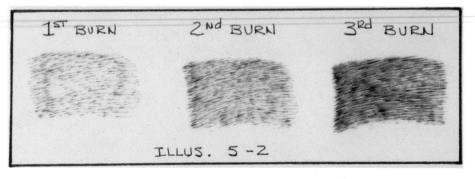

1ˢᵀ BURN   2ᴺᵈ BURN   3ᴿᵈ BURN

ILLUS. 5-2

The first, second, and third burns for making natural-looking fur.

Sand off the ridges after burning each layer of fur.

Brush the surface clean with a brass wire brush. See how much lighter the surface becomes.

Burn the second layer of fur-lines.

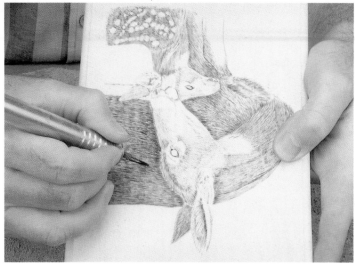

This is the wrong way to hold the picture as you work on this fur section.

Instead, hold it so that you can work easily in the direction of the hair growth. Hold the pen comfortably, so that it aligns with your arm.

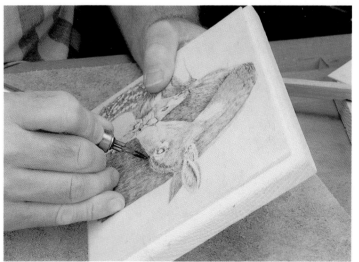

Elevate the piece to avoid rising heat from reaching your fingers.

Close up of the second burn. Again, the rippled look is caused by the grain of the wood, not by short, overlapping burn-lines. Soft areas of the grain burn darker than hard areas.

Brass-brushing the third burn of the fur. Do not sand.

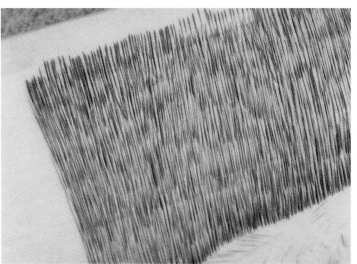

Sand and brush the second burn layer, so that it appears light again, and the line details are clear.

In areas of fur that have a lot of contour, like the chest of the deer, use short strokes so you can vary the direction easily.

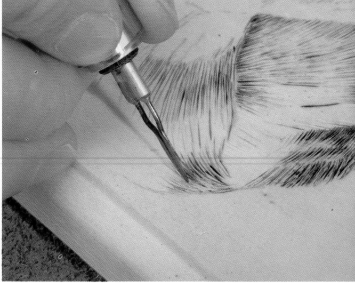

The third burn is used to create dark shadows wherever they are needed, and to create texture. Burn these lines in slight diagonals to the previous lines, to fill in the shading. Light and dark striped effects caused by the underlying grain can be eliminated by going over the lighter areas.

Working with short strokes on curves and contours.

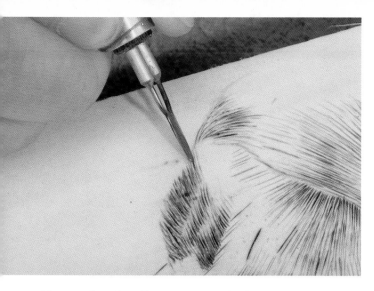

Short strokes also allow you to get detailed shading.

Here are some good examples of hair- and fur-burning techniques from the works of Charles Gardner. Note in the Lab how the burn marks follow the curves and contours of the skin folds. Also, compare the short burn strokes used on the face of the Lab, where the hair is finer, with the longer strokes used on the body of the Shepherd, where it is coarser.

Other points to note are the flat-edge burning technique used on the Shepherd's nose, use of black marker and highlighting of eye pupils.

A German Shepherd, by Charles Gardner.

A Labrador, by Charles Gardner.

FEATHERS

More than anything else, good pen control is the key to producing realistic feathers, as well as attention to details such as vane contours and splits. Once you have become proficient at rolling or rotating the pen in your fingers, you shouldn't have any problems.

Assuming you have your pattern traced or penciled on the work piece, start by creating the exposed quills with two condescending lines. Once your quills are outlined, you may raise them for effect by using the flat-edge technique and burning on the outside of the quill. I prefer to use one of the angled shaped square ended tips for this. When raising the quill in this fashion, try to be as consistent as possible by doing one side with a smooth stroke from start to finish. Pausing during the stroke or trying to raise one side of the quill with several short strokes will leave you with an uneven burn. I always like to go back over the burns by lightly sanding them with a very fine grit paper. I am careful not to sand off the raised quill, by folding the paper and sanding up to and against the outside of the quill. This will help to smooth out the high and low places which may have developed.

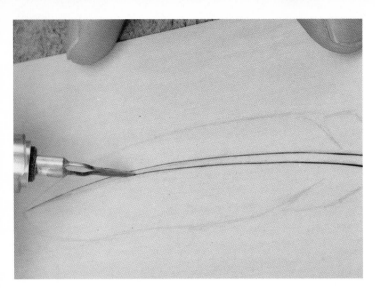

Condescending quill lines taper together towards the tip of the feather. Burn the quill borders with a straight-edged pen.

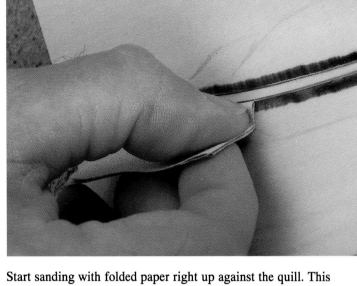

Start sanding with folded paper right up against the quill. This lightens the color of the burn, and also takes out any uneven ridges and bumps left by the flat-edge pen.

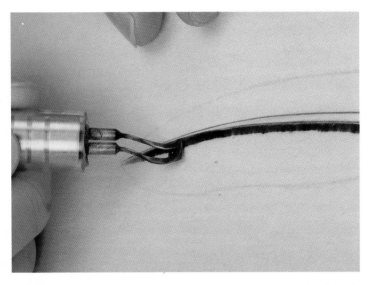

Then return with a flat-edge pen and burn along both borders. I am applying more pressure on the inside edge, along the quill line, as you can see by the slant of the flat pen tip.

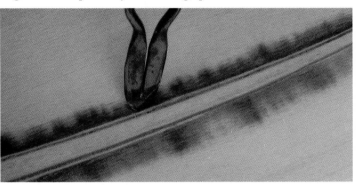

The technique creates a raised quill, which will be much easier to paint if you choose to do so later.

Very realistic carved feathers can be made the same way. First, draw in your quill lines, condescending at the end.

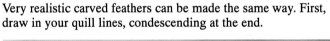

Then again, on the opposite side of the quill.

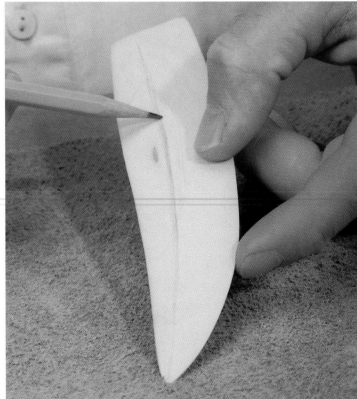

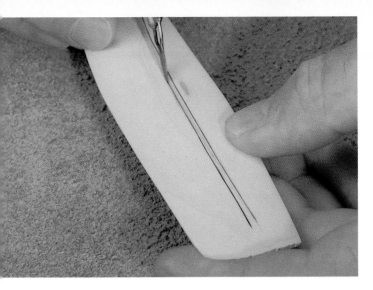

Burn in the quill borders.

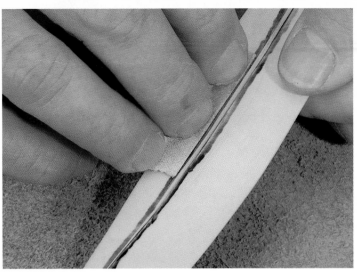

Sand, with the sandpaper right up against the quill wall. This will smooth out any ridges, and lighten the color of the burn.

You can use the flat side of a pointed pen tip if you don't have a flat-edge tip to raise the quill. Keep the point of the tip up to the quill wall.

Once this step is complete, brush and dust it before burning in the vanes. Pencil in some guide mark for vane directions before burning the vanes. Right-handers should burn from left to right when burning the vanes, and just the opposite for southpaws. This allows for better visibility when placing the tip for subsequent strokes. Your spacing of the vanes will be more accurate and consistent.

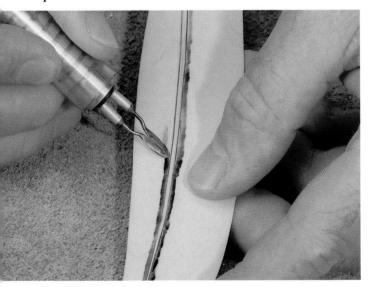

Do the same for the second side.

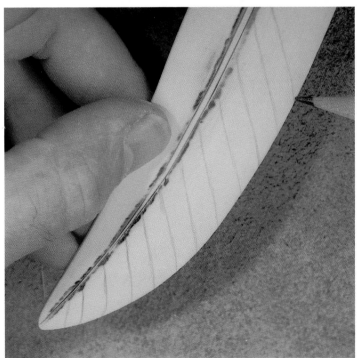

Pencil in some guide marks for the feather vanes.

Burn in the vanes. I burn left to right for consistency, since I am right-handed -- it makes it easier to see the next spot for placing my pen tip, without my hands getting in the way. Left-handers should burn right to left.

For burning vanes, I like to use a pointed or spear shaped tip. This allows me to start my vane burns right against the side of the quill. Start burning the vanes next to the quill, pulling the pen tip towards the edge of the feather. Don't forget to roll the pen in your fingers to create the curves and contours. Very seldom will a feather have straight vanes. Keep in mind the burn lines themselves are not the vanes. The vanes are the ridge lines created between the burns.

This is an important thought to keep while creating feathers. It's worth repeating to say that paying attention to detail and studying the particular characteristics are vital to creating realistic looking feathers.

For realism and interest, add some feather contours,

and splits, like these on the feather I burned on illustration board.

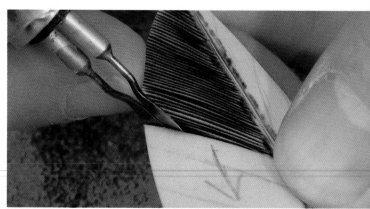

To make a feather split in an individual carved feather, burn one of your lines all the way through the wood, as close to the quill as you'd like the split to extend. Remember that the lines you are burning are not the vanes themselves -- they are the spaces between the vanes, and a split is just a slightly bigger space. Keep in mind that they should change the angle of the surrounding vanes a little bit.

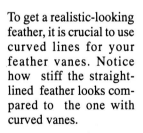

To get a realistic-looking feather, it is crucial to use curved lines for your feather vanes. Notice how stiff the straight-lined feather looks compared to the one with curved vanes.

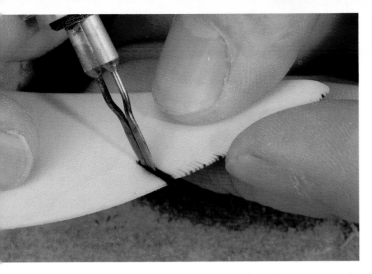

Clean up the split by burning the inside edges from the opposite side.

For these smaller feathers, I chose to suggest the quills using only a single line.

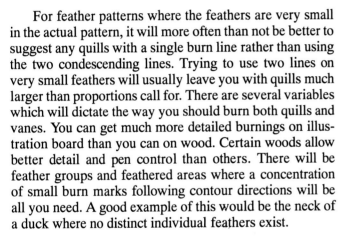

For feather patterns where the feathers are very small in the actual pattern, it will more often than not be better to suggest any quills with a single burn line rather than using the two condescending lines. Trying to use two lines on very small feathers will usually leave you with quills much larger than proportions call for. There are several variables which will dictate the way you should burn both quills and vanes. You can get much more detailed burnings on illustration board than you can on wood. Certain woods allow better detail and pen control than others. There will be feather groups and feathered areas where a concentration of small burn marks following contour directions will be all you need. A good example of this would be the neck of a duck where no distinct individual feathers exist.

Here, on the other hand, I used double-line quills.

The many shapes of feathers that appear on even just one bird can be a major challenge. You will need to pay close attention to details and be a keen observer of how they may differ from one another and group to group.

More about burning feathers in the section discussing three-dimensional work.

THREE-DIMENSIONAL WORK

For you carvers, the added difficulty of burning a contoured surface versus a flat one will be present. It will be necessary to slightly rotate the workpiece in your hand while you also rotate the pen in your fingers, so that you can accommodate the contoured areas and maintain line direction accurately.

In bird-carving, there will be occasions when both top and underside of a feather—like an extended primary feather—will need to be burned. You will want to duplicate exactly the same pattern on the bottom as you have on the top. This will really add quality to your piece, and it is not difficult to do. A method I have found to work well calls for laying a piece of paper over the finished top side and rubbing over it with a pencil to create a pattern on paper. The illustrations here will show you how to proceed.

The vanes have been finished on the front of this feather, and I am ready to begin on the underside. To make sure the vanes match up on the opposite sides, I use a paper tracing.

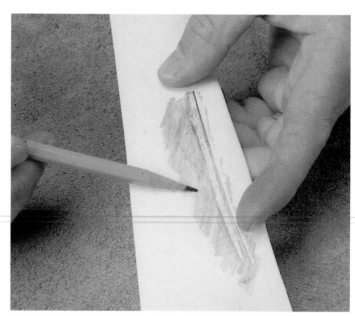

When you are burning on a three-dimensional carved piece like this one, you will find it easier to get a smooth line if you hold the burning tool still and rotate the piece itself.

Place the paper over the burned side of the feather, and use a pencil to make a rubbing of the vanes, just like you did with a penny as a kid, to get a picture of Abe Lincoln's face.

The finished rubbing should show the vaneing pattern.

Use the burning tool to cut out the feather splits.

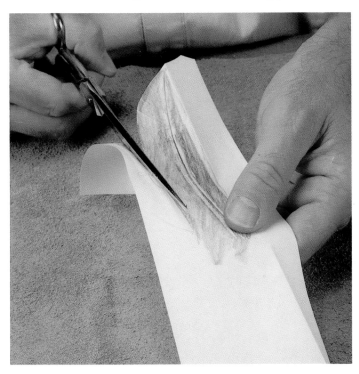

Use scissors and cut out the rubbing pattern.

Also use your burning tool to cut in random guidelines in the vaneing.

41

The finished paper feather guide.

The carved feather is now marked with feather splits and vane directions patterned after the reverse side.

Turn the pattern over, and line up the paper feather splits with the ones on the blank side of the carved wooden feather. Tape them together.

Use a pencil to mark splits and guides onto the feather by drawing in the cuts of the paper.

You can now draw in any additional guidelines you think might be helpful, including the quill lines.

Now you can burn the underside of the feather. Burn vaneing around the splits and contours first. Then you can continue with the rest of the vanes and finish the feather. You should end up with a vaneing pattern on the underside that matches the top side.

BLACK AND WHITE SUBJECTS

Some of the more difficult challenges in your pyrographic efforts will come when trying to depict a white or black subject, with white subjects being the least forgiving. I learned a great deal about this when I tried to depict a Snowy Owl in clear hard maple. After many hours of work, I abandoned the project, leaving myself with experience gained as the only fruit of my efforts. More often than not, when the subject is white, it's what you don't burn that counts the most. Contain your detailing to areas of the subject that are not white or those being shadowed. Remember that light or white obliterates. On the areas of a white subject where the light is to appear most direct, at the very most, only lightly suggest an outline. In many cases, don't burn anything. Let the mind's eye of the viewer complete the image.

On this chick's head, you can see how I used small lines to indicate feather contour. I have been sparing with detail, to keep the area light-colored.

I've used small lines on this swan's face, again for feather contour. Here it was alright for the area to darken somewhat, so I used more lines.

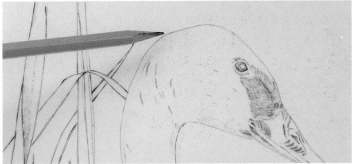

The head of the swan was done correctly, with only a broken line at the top of the head, and mere suggestions of the feather directions.

When you are portraying white subjects, it is very tricky to show light-reflecting areas and shading. On this illustration-board pyrograph of a swan and her chicks, you can see what I did right—and what I did wrong.

Under the chin, where a shadow would fall naturally, more detail can be shown.

In areas that would normally be shaded (like the inside curve of this blade of grass), I have applied some detail. The outside, which is exposed to the light, reveals no detail at all, as if they have been washed out by the brightness.

On stained pieces, outlines of light-reflecting areas can be created by a sanding process described in Chapter Six. On white birds, burn in a few feather splits in the areas exposed to direct light. This will create the illusion of shadows and greatly enhance your creations.

Black objects generally absorb the light, and shadows are nearly invisible. The only exception is shiny areas of a black subject such as a slick-haired cat or the nose of a dog. I have found the use of a waterproof marker invaluable in aiding me in these areas. I burn the black areas for texture, and then dye them with the marker after brushing out the char. It's amazing what a black marker can do for a piece when used on things like noses, eyes, claws, and black tips.

Unfortunately, too much detailing on the back eliminated the whiteness I wanted to achieve. I should have used a more suggestive burning style.

The unburned and lightly burned areas on this chick create the light-reflecting highpoints of the head. Notice that the lines defining the chin, where shadows should fall, are much darker than those at the top of the head. As you burn, think about how light would fall on the actual subject. Also note the solid lines in the swan's breast feathers. Solid lines are a 'no-no', especially in this case.

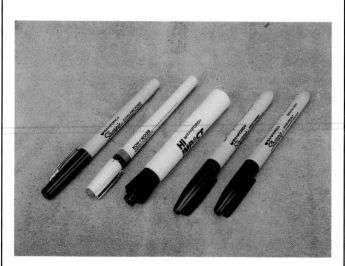

I use a variety of pens to add details in black.

"Coon Hollow" makes good use of sanded highlights and black-inked details on the faces, and light-colored sanded edges on the ears.

A detail of "Coon Hollow."

TREES & LANDSCAPES

Trees, shrubs, grasses, weeds, etc., most often look best with a more suggestive style of burning. They are not usually the primary subject matter and details should be kept to a minimum so as not to detract from the main subject. One exception to this is when they are in the extreme foreground of your pattern, for the purpose of creating the illusion of depth. In this case, detail is important so it will appear close to the viewer's eye.

I have often used the pointed pen tips to make dots to create a clump of leaves on a branch (stippling). In any suggestive patterning of greenery, concentrate on the light source and the shadows it creates. Almost any type of pattern will work if you have done well with your reflections and shadows. It will look well if you mix up your patterns to include several different types of trees. Even from a distance, pine trees look much different than poplar trees, for example.

As you progress further into the foreground, start indicating the trunks and limbs, and as you progress even further, put some bark texturing on them and start indicating the actual shape of the leaves. At your first opportunity, step outside and get very near a tree or shrub. Take a few moments to study what your eyes see at close range, and then take a look at trees and shrubs far away. You'll come back in with a clearer understanding of this lesson.

Grasses are depicted only in extreme foregrounds. Don't try to put grass blades on a distant knoll. It will look better to have nothing more than a flat edge burn to indicate a knoll. If you want to depict tall grasses or weeds at a distance, do so sparingly with one or two here and there. Low lying areas such as old road beds can be indicated well with flat edge shadowing. They can be accented with some of the finishing instructions in Chapter Six.

The distant tree-line I burned for this piece shows many textures you may want to use. This pattern originated from a photograph, and was used to decorate a maplewood box. The cabin, property, and box all belong to Yolanda Green in Floyd County, Ga.

45

A sample of foreground and background foliage patterns. Note how detail diminishes to create an illusion of depth.

Bricks are a useful texture for many illustrations you may want to try. Use the calligraphy pen with its square tip to make small bricks.

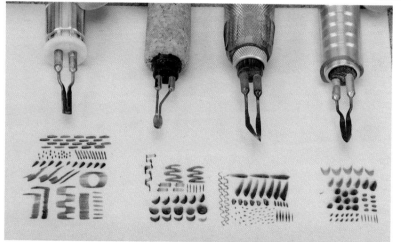

You can achieve a multitude of effects by angling your tips in difference ways. It is worth your time to experiment, and make some "samplers" of techniques like this one.

You will find that it is more effective to suggest the all-over pattern than to fill in each and every brick. The width of the tip may be a limiting factor if its proportions do not match your intended bricks.

BRICKS

When depicting brick or stone, don't burn in the joints. Burn the brick or stone, and the joints will create themselves. This usually requires some layout with a pencil before starting. Don't try to put every brick or stone in the wall of a building. Put just enough patches of your pattern in to indicate that the wall is brick. In most scenes the brick will nearly be obscure because they are so small relative to the rest of the subject matter. In these situations it is easy to overdo it or make them too big. You will get a better effect by scantily using the sharp edge of a pointed tip, holding the pen at a high angle. This will require a lower operating temperature, as you use a barely-touching motion.

A tip that works especially well for brick patterning is a calligraphy pen tip, but you may be limited if its size is not proportionate to your work. If the calligraphy pen is larger than your pattern calls for, you can tilt it and burn with one of it's corner edges for a smaller burn. It you need larger bricks, you can use a flat-edge pen.

Use a flat-edge pen to burn in brick patterns between joint lines.

MORE HELPFUL HINTS

There may be times when you need to make use of a straight edge. A metal-edged ruler doesn't work well because it absorbs most of the heat before it gets to the work piece. Use glass or a ceramic straight-edge instead.

Charles Gardner's architectural renderings in wood shown here are good examples of pieces in which distinct lines and a straight edge worked well. Note the attention given to the old house, and how the long shadows of the trees in front of the church give a late evening calm to the scene.

Wherever it is possible, try to incorporate any unwanted burnmarks into your pattern scheme. If the mistake is too obvious to camoflage, you might be able to cut it out, but the results of your corrective measures will be noticeable. Unfortunately, no matter what material you are burning on, whether leather, wood, or paper, very little can be done to correct major mistakes. The primary cause of mistakes is imcomplete planning and hurrying the project, so take your time and use your pencil.

For larger bricks, draw the pattern (with the mortar dividers) first.

An entire book could be written on this subject alone. As a matter of fact, there are numerous books on the subject of wood finishing without regard to finishing a piece with a pyrographed pattern. I make no claims of being an expert on stains, sealers, varnishes, oils or acrylic coatings, which can produce an unknown number of different effects on different types of wood. However, I can share with you some simple techniques which have worked well for me. Before getting down to the final coat, let's complete our pyrograph.

UNSTAINED PIECES

The simplest projects are those which require no stain or paint. Use a fine grain sanding paper such as 180 or 220 grit and lightly remove the rough surfaces caused by the burns. On some hardwoods (such as maple) I have used 100 or 120 grit paper on an orbital sander, which will do it very fast. After sanding, use a soft bristle brush and thoroughly clean out the dust and char by going with the direction of your burn strokes where possible. Brush and wipe it clean.

Now it's ready for the finish, and the choice is yours. I like a non-yellowing clear acrylic spray in a satin finish. The satin finish has less glare so the pyrographic details can be seen from almost any angle. You can also use a rub-on tung oil, which will really bring out the grain, but it takes no less than three coats and darkens the wood a bit. Also, it usually takes a day to dry between coats.

FINISHING WITH STAIN

I really enjoy staining my pieces, because I can add so much more to them. There are certain woods which will not work well for these purposes–almost always the softer, porous and more absorbent woods. Never use a dark stain on an end-grain cut, such as rounds with bark around the edges. The stain is absorbed deeply and darkens the wood so much that it obliterates the pattern.

I certainly haven't tried every stain on the market, but one of my favorites is a #40 Cherry by Red Devil. This stain is thick and easy to apply. The wood doesn't seem to absorb it as deep or as fast as some of the other brands. It has a medium darkness which contrasts well with both the burned areas and the highlighted areas.

I usually just wipe it on and off with a rag. How dark it stains depends on a couple of factors. Primarily the wood will determine this, though the grit of paper used to prepare the surface will have its effects also: a coarser grit will leave a darker finish.

To give yourself a good idea of this effect, sand a board with 80 grit paper, and finish one half of it with 100 grit, the other with 150 grit. When you stain the board, you should see quite a contrast between the two areas, with the 100 grit side being the darkest. As you can see, there are many variables for stains. Only you can determine what suits your needs and tastes. Don't be afraid to experiment a little; you will learn a lot with little effort. Use some of your scrap pieces of lumber for these tests.

When you have completely burned your piece, it is ready to stain, providing you have cleaned out your burns.

Cover it thickly,

and completely, with a liberal dose of stain.

Do not forget to coat the edges.

Immediately wipe it clean with a paper towel, removing as much of the stain as possible. Initially, you may think that you have just ruined your project, but don't be alarmed–all will be O.K.

After the piece dries somewhat, you will be ready to add the finishing touches–highlights and shadows. It does not have to be completely dry for you to begin these steps.

HIGHLIGHTING STAINED PIECES

By removing the stain in certain areas of my pyrograph, I can create a more three dimensional look and enhance the light-reflecting areas of my subject. After I am done with all of the burning, I apply a coat of stain and immediately wipe it off with a clean, dust-free cloth, allowing it to dry for 10 to 12 hours. Then I spray a thin coat of fast-drying clear polyurethane spray to seal in the stain, so it won't bleed back into the areas I want to highlight. On softer woods such as basswood, I scrape and highlight immediately after staining without sealing it first. My favorite wood for applying stain is maple. It's very hard and allows me to recover the original light color with little difficulty.

Once dry, I use a sharp edged knife blade to scrape away the areas I want to look white or light in color. This is done quite easily and doesn't require an enormous amount of pressure. The knife blade should be held at a 90 degree angle or less to the surface. Never angle it so that the cutting edge slants in the direction you are scraping.

Try to soften the edges where it calls for it, such as rounded or curved areas. Once you have completed scraping, soften everything up with fine grit sanding paper or triple-ought steel wool, especially on those areas where the light and dark blend together. Check your work to see if it looks good and clean. Finish with two or three more coats of polyurethane spray, being sure it's lightly buffed between each coat with the triple ought steel wool.

Once the stain is dry, you can highlight the white parts as I have done on the deer, by scratching and scraping the finish off. A pointed, curved blade works best for scraping.

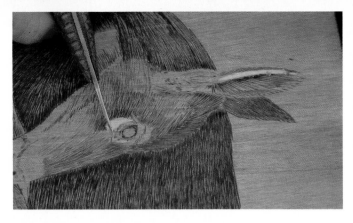

The edges of the ear and under the eye,

the muzzle,

and under the neck are white places I scraped.

A straight, narrow-pointed blade is useful for scraping whiskers, eyelashes, etc.

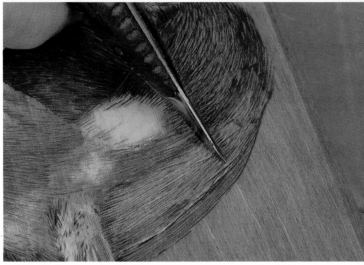

Less scraping is required to add highlights to areas with fur that reflects light.

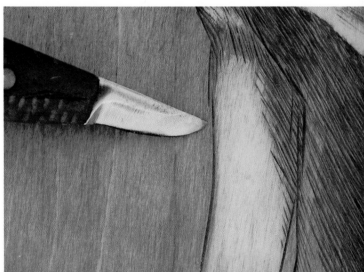

Create a rounded effect by scraping some areas completely white, like the front of this leg, but leaving other areas slightly stained.

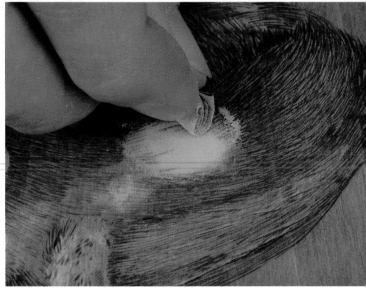

Use sandpaper or steel wool to soften up the highlights,

The highlighting and scraping process is completed on this basswood pyrograph plaque.

Another version of the swan pattern. This one on wood, shows how useful scraping can be on a large scale. The black details, done with a dye marker, give it a finishing touch. Collection of Mr. Guerry Thorton, Atlanta, GA.

Use black markers to darken the eyes and the noses.

This dogwood plaque uses scraping in the white areas of the flowers, and on the rounded, highlighted areas of the leaves. Collection of Mrs. Debra Michalek, Poway, CA.

If you are planning to stain your project, keep that in mind while burning your pattern. You will see things in your pattern which will be better depicted by scraping than by burning. A good example would be in the white edges around the ears of certain animals. In most cases, even if the hair is not actually white, it appears white because of the light reflection. By using the sharp pointed edges of a knife, you can quickly etch in these hair lines through the stain providing your wood is light colored. This works really well on whiskers. The trick is to do it in one quick scratching motion. Practice this before actually trying it on your work piece.

Scraping a few other areas will help bring your subjects to life—particularly the eyes and noses. Once you have darkened them with the waterproof black marker, highlight the reflections by scraping. Also, scrape highlights on the top edges of limbs (or anywhere else in your pattern where the reflections dictate) to help suggest their roundness. My only caution is not to get too carried away on the subjects and areas which are not the pattern's primary subject.

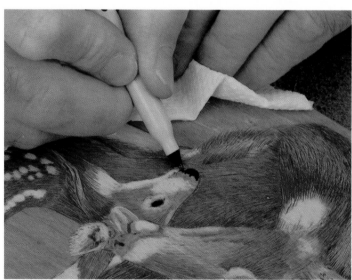

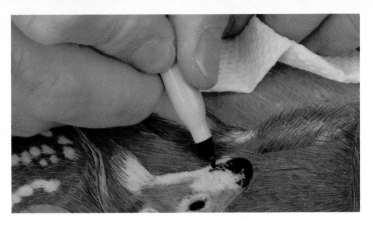

You can use a stippling technique for some areas.

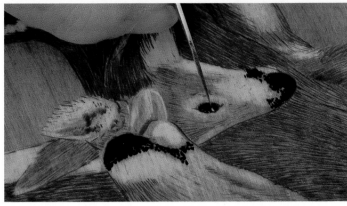

Add a little sparkle to the eye by etching out a small dot to indicate a light spot.

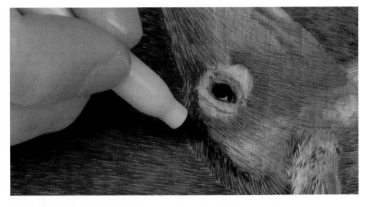

A few dark streaks can add extra depth.

Do the same to add a little shine to the nose.

Dark streaks along the back (made with a broader-tipped pen) will be softened later to add contour.

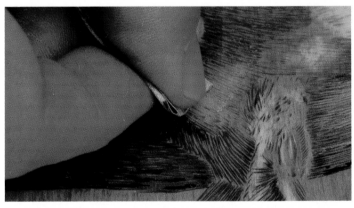

Use sandpaper or steel wool to soften up the highlights, and to blend the black details.

Scraping these lightly softens them, and makes them less streaky in appearance.

Gently, use a brass brush to remove dust and particles created by the blending process.

After checking to make sure that all is satisfactory, I use a clear wood finish with a semi-gloss surface to seal my piece.

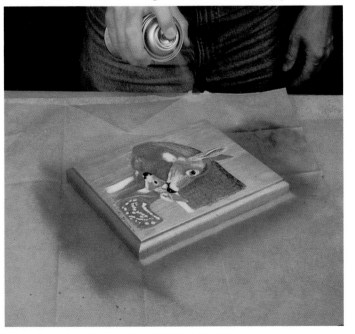

Follow the directions from whatever brand you use, and coat the entire piece.

The finished piece, now in the collection of Leslie Bockol, who photographed its creation.

ADDING COLOR

I have on occasions added color to some of my pieces, but usually only when a customer requests it or if I feel I need to accent the piece with just a little color here or there. I have some reservations about adding color because it can take away from the true art form. This is with respect to flat art pieces on wood and not carvings, nor do I consider staining to be in this category. For the purpose of this lesson, I'm making reference to the use of paints, dyes and waterproof markers.

A good rule of thumb for adding color is transparency. If you can still see the wood grain through the color, your woodburning will not suffer as much loss of the pyrographic art form. If you use too much coloring, you end up with a painting on wood which has been merely textured with a pyrographic pen. If you use acrylic or oil paints, be sure you apply them in thin coats, and only where you think it's absolutely necessary. A touch of color in the eyes of a bird or cat or on a flower may be all you need. There may be an area in your piece which seems to be camouflaged by the surrounding areas which needs some emphasis by coloring.

When I do add color, I often use the waterproof markers. Sometimes I will have to lightly scrape these spots with my knife because the color is too loud. This tones it down yet still leaves enough color for effect.

A pet portrait. Collection of Sheryn Faro, Atlanta, GA.

Adding color to a pyrograph must be done sparingly. Charles Gardner did well with this one. Note the thin scattered blotches of blue in the sky. Even in the water the wood is still exposed in large part.

Collection of Leslie Wells, Lawrenceville, GA.

Collection of Jim Newbill, Atlanta, GA.

Chee-chee's on a maple box. Collection of Mr. & Mrs. Ted Higgins, Marietta, GA.

OBJECTS FOR BURNING

In addition to wooden plaques you can buy or make, there are numerous other items you can decorate with your burning pen. Anything made out of wood without a finish already on it can be decorated—boxes, spice racks, napkin holders, wood spoons, gun stocks, gun cabinet doors, wooden plates, walking sticks, wooden jewelry, Christmas ornaments and whatever else you can think of. In addition to wooden items, you can burn on leather, paper, plastic, fungus, gourds, cork and other materials. There are many items made from these materials as well.

LEATHER BURNING

I have found leather to be a wonderful material to burn on. Leathers come in a variety of colors, textures, thickness, and finishes. Using your burning pen with the flat edge technique on the leather with a slightly textured surface can create some interesting effects and patterns. It requires little if any preparation and the pen tip slides smoothly over the surface. It will burn very light or very dark, and does so with relatively low operating temperatures. The only drawback is the expense of the leather. You can buy smaller precut items such as wallets, belts, key chains, etc., which are not too expensive, and personalize them for gifts or to sell.

I burned a wild turkey fan feather on this turkey box call made by Mr. Billy Buice of Canton, GA.

A maple box with a curled-up fawn. This piece was finished unstained.

This whitetailed buck worked well on tan-colored leather.

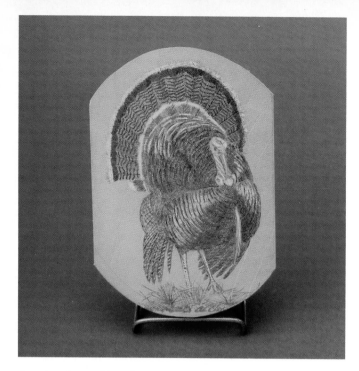

A turkey burned into leather. To make a secure, flat work surface, I glued the piece of leather to a board before burning it.

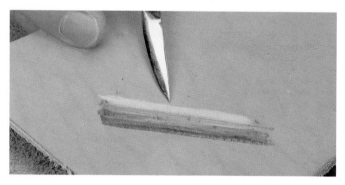

Burning and scraping can be used to achieve many different effects in leather-burning.

PAPER BURNING

Burning on paper has tremendous possibilities because there are so many textures, colors, and varieties. On professional stock such as acid free ragboard, you can add color washes and really be creative. The ragboard is relatively inexpensive compared to wood and leather. You might suspect a lower operating temperature for burning on paper, but usually just the opposite is the case.

Burning on brown paper bags and other relatively thick papers can be an adventure all its own. You can use the sharp-edge burning pens much as you would a sharp-edged knife to cut out stencils or paper parts. You will be amazed at how easy it is to cut the paper with a hot tip. It's much faster than with a knife or scissors and the cuts are clean and crisp. Start out on a lower temperature setting, increasing the temperature gradually until your pen cuts through the paper without charring the edges. Paper feathers, leaves, dolls, etc., are easily made this way. Once they are detailed with your burning pen, you can cut them out as mentioned and place them on different colored backgrounds for some interesting effects. If you are so inclined, you can make some beautiful collages and works of art using this technique. Try different colors of paper and add pen and ink for contrasts and accents. There is really no limit to what you can create.

You can also make items such as leaves and feathers more realistic by shaping them with one of your pen tips. To do this, use the flat-edge technique to iron the piece, which will cause it to curl or bend upward. You can actually shape it to curve both from end to end and side to side. A little practice is all you'll need to get the hang of it. It's a very simple process. Spray these type pieces with a clear sealer for added strength. On the larger pieces (4" length or width) try using an iron to get the shapes you want.

A bald eagle, burned on a gray-colored piece of leather, which has a slight texture to it. Note that I shaded behind he eagle's white head for better clarity.

Using the flat side of the burning tip, create a crease down the middle.

Making pyrography designs on paper is not much different from working on wood or leather. To start out, use a pencil to draw a leaf, feather, or any other image you'd like to burn. I am making a leaf from a brown paper grocery bag.

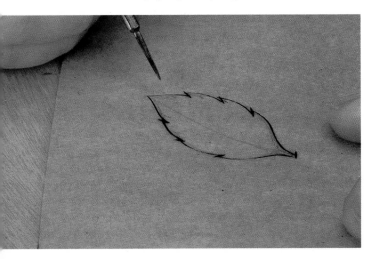

Use the flat edge again to add the vanes.

Use a sharp-edged burning pen to cut the outline.

To give the leaf a natural curve, use the flat edge to 'iron' it. Go straight up the center, covering its entire length.

Once the outline has been burned, you should be able to lift it out easily.

Now do the same working from the center out to the edge between each of the veins.

After a little practice, you will be able to make cupped leaves that look very real.

See how much detail you can put into a paper feather? Both of these were made from a brown paper bag. The feather on the right was accented with a fine-tipped black marker.

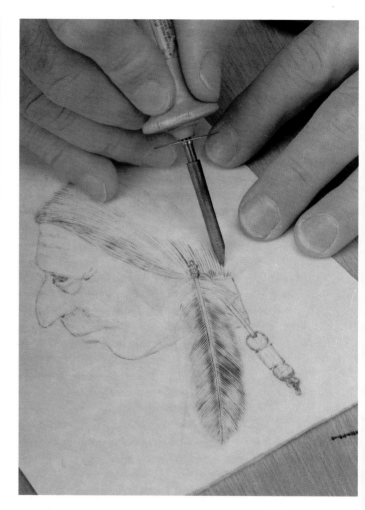

A piece of scotch tape on the back will reinforce and stiffen your paper feathers.

Parchment paper gives an antique look to this Indian. I folded this paper in half to prevent burn-throughs, since this is very thin stock. If you do have burn-throughs, just back your piece with another sheet of the same stock.

GOURDS

There are some artisans whose primary pyrography is done on gourds. Again, there is a lot of room for creativity in this area alone, so let your imagination run free. Not only can you burn your patterns onto gourds, you can cut them into pieces and rejoin them to make interesting and useful objects or decor pieces.

Photographs of Works by
Malcolm (Mack) Freeman

Gourd burnings by Malcolm "Mack" Freeman of Harlem, Ga.

These freehanded burnings on uniquely crafted gourds make for beautiful decor items. Mack states he uses a 25 Watt system with a wedged shape tip almost exclusively. He also notes that because each gourd is different in shape and color you can duplicate patterns on different gourds and have uniquely different results. The finished product compliments most any decor.

Mack is quite an authority on gourds and welcomes any inquiries.

Photographs by Christina Manning

Conclusion

Now that you have a better idea of what pyrography is all about, all you need to do is start burning and be creative. If you have a fondness or special attraction for a particular subject, I recommend you try burning it. Whether it's old farm scenes, dogs, birds, or whatever, your special interests will go far in helping you to develop your own style. No matter what material you burn on, there are many roads your burning pen can travel. This can be a wonderful and exciting adventure of creativity and I wish you much success.

Another pet portrait. Collection of Sheryn Faro, Atlanta, GA.

A pet portrait. Collection of Sheryn Faro, Atlanta, GA.

Eastern Tom. Collection of Dale Bailey, Macon, GA.

Buglin' Bull Moose. Collection of Dale Bailey, Macon, GA.

One of three Gordon County, GA courthouse pyrographs. This one is in the collection of Mr. & Mrs. L. C. Stephens, Calhoun, GA.

This detail of a whitetail buck I carved (10" long from nose to tail) shows how I created the fine hair texture on his face and neck with the use of a burning pen. The buck is in the collection of Mr. & Mrs. James Durham, Acworth, GA.

A flying turkey I carved, and then detailed with pyrogrphy.

Detail of a turkey in flight, showing textures and feathering done with burning tools.

No doubt, once this book goes to press, I will think of or discover something I wish I had included. You too will discover helpful and easier ways not found in this book. Pyrography has endless possibilities, and its creative powers are limited only by the artist's imagination. It is highly unlikely that one person could become the absolute authority on pyrography given so many materials and objects to apply it to. Combined with the new and innovative equipment which keeps coming our way, I believe it will soon be written about in specialized areas of interests, including burning on leather, gourds, paper, etc.

A carved turkey detailed with burning tools.

Details of the standing turkey.

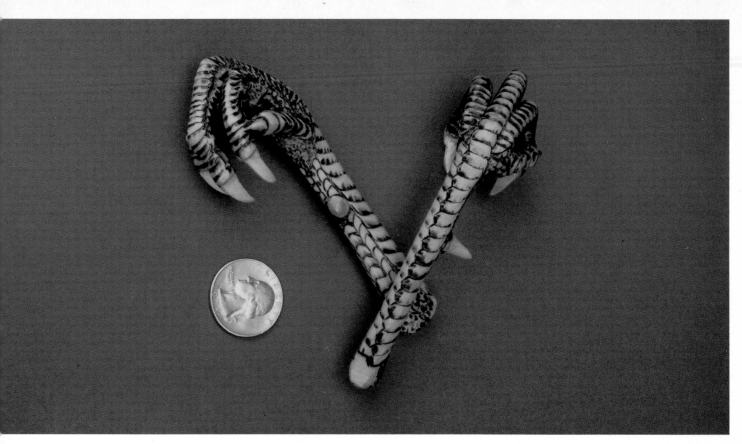

Two turkey claws: carved, burned, and ready to be added to a finished turkey carving. I used a burning pen to create the raised and reliefed skin scales on the legs and toes.

Even carvings as small as this wood duck pin can be greatly enhanced with the use of a burning pen to add details.

Suppliers Directory

BURNING SYSTEMS

Leisure Time Produces, Inc.
(Detail Master)
2650 Davisson Street
River Grove, Ill. 60171
(708) 452-5400

Nibsburner
3255 Blue Mountain Way
Colorado Springs, Co. 80906
(719) 576-8686

Colwood Electronics, Inc.
Dept. WCC
15 Meridian Rd.
Eatontown, N.J. 07724
(908) 544-1119

Navesink Electronics
381 Nutswamp Rd.
Red Bank, N.J. 07701
(908) 747-5023

BOOKS AND WOODBURNING PRODUCTS

Claudia Nice Books (pen & ink drawings)
Susan Schewee Publications
13454 NE Whitaker Way
Portland, Oregon 97230
(503) 254-9100

Walnut Hollow Farm
(press-on patterns, plaques,
basswood rounds, plates)
1978 Walnut Hollow Farms,Inc.
R2, Dodgeville, Wi. 53533

Wemakint (Mr. Dick Baker)
(plates, round boxes,
made from basswood)
R.R. 6, Box 6675B
Cleveland, Ga. 30528
(706) 865-6705

Herb's Yellowstone
(knife sharpening compound)
1041 Utterback Road
Great Falls, VA 22066
(703) 450-5985